GREEK

MYTHOLOGY

GODS AND HEROES BROUGHT TO LIFE

For Nicole, Nikita, and Nikki with love

GREEK
MYTHOLOGY
GODS AND HEROES BROUGHT TO LIFE

ROBERT GARLAND

PEN & SWORD **HISTORY**

AN IMPRINT OF PEN & SWORD BOOKS LTD.
YORKSHIRE – PHILADELPHIA

First published in Great Britain in 2020 by
PEN AND SWORD HISTORY
An imprint of
Pen & Sword Books Ltd
Yorkshire - Philadelphia

Copyright © Robert Garland, 2020

ISBN 978 1 52677 654 9

Typeset in Times New Roman 11.5/14 by
SJmagic DESIGN SERVICES, India.
Printed and bound in the UK by CPI Books, Ltd.

Pen & Sword Books Ltd incorporates the Imprints of Pen & Sword Books
Archaeology, Atlas, Aviation, Battleground, Discovery, Family History, History,
Maritime, Military, Naval, Politics, Railways, Select, Transport, True Crime,
Fiction, Frontline Books, Leo Cooper, Praetorian Press, Seaforth Publishing,
Wharncliffe and White Owl.

For a complete list of Pen & Sword titles please contact
PEN & SWORD BOOKS LIMITED
47 Church Street, Barnsley, South Yorkshire, S70 2AS, England
E-mail: enquiries@pen-and-sword.co.uk
Website: www.pen-and-sword.co.uk

Or
PEN AND SWORD BOOKS
1950 Lawrence Rd, Havertown, PA 19083, USA
E-mail: Uspen-and-sword@casematepublishers.com
Website: www.penandswordbooks.com

Contents

Acknowledgements

I would never have begun drawing without the inspiration and friendship of Mike Goldmark, my guide and mentor in the world of art. As always, I also want to pay tribute to Sir Mick Jagger for his indefatigability and invincibility.

Introduction

Monsters with a single eye in the centre of their forehead, heroes who travel to the ends of the earth, sons who marry their mothers, sons who kill their fathers, sons who castrate their fathers, fathers who eat their children, goddesses who turn men into stags so they are hunted by their own hounds for being peeping toms, trios of women with a single eye and a single tooth between them, artists who fall in love with their own creation – what's not to like?

Greek mythology isn't the equivalent of the Tanakh or the New Testament or the Qur'an or the Hindu Bhagavad Gita or the Vedic Upanishads. Even though the gods are prominent, there's nothing sacred about it. So, for example, the story of the birth of Zeus doesn't have anything like the same religious significance for the Greeks as the story of the birth of Jesus does for Christians.

There is no standardised version of any myth. *Muthos* in Greek simply means 'story'. All we have to go on for our sources is a hotchpotch of highly unrepresentative writings produced by some of the least typical minds of their time – a period, incidentally, lasting well over a thousand years – whose perspective is likely to have been somewhat idiosyncratic, to say the least. These sources include the poems of Homer and Hesiod, the *Histories* of Herodotus, the plays of the tragedians Aeschylus, Sophocles and Euripides, the comedies of Aristophanes, the dialogues of Plato, Ovid's epic masterpiece the *Metamorphoses*, and a compilation of myths by a certain Apollodorus called *The Library*.

Those who will be speaking in their own words are the gods and the heroes. In case you haven't noticed, the gods are everywhere. They're in your body, in your head, in the weather, in the crops, in the seasons, on the battlefield, in your home, in your city or village, out at sea, in streams and rivers, and in what you eat and drink.

Homer.

The only human experience they steer clear of is – wait for it – death, and that's because death is a source of pollution and the gods must remain pure and uncorrupted. Don't expect any words of consolation when you're just about to snuff it, therefore. Once you're dead, you'll descend to Hades and enter the realm of Pluto and Persephone, however good or bad you've been. We all end up in the same place, saints and sinners, in other words. Pluto and Persephone will be down there with you, not that they'll have anything to do with you or even give you the time of day.

The Greek gods are anthropomorphic, which means they have human shapes, human drives, and human appetites. The only difference between their appetites and ours is that theirs are much, much bigger. They do all the things we do: eat, drink, sleep and have sex. They also lie, cheat, steal and commit acts of violence on a routine basis. Though they'll live forever, they exist inside the universe, which means they're immanent, not transcendent. They aren't therefore responsible for creation. They were born, or at least came into being, just like us.

They don't age or fall sick. Each of them is stuck at a specific moment in her or his life cycle. Zeus is forever middle-aged, Apollo is forever a young man at the peak of his fitness and strength, Artemis is forever a young girl on the cusp of womanhood, and so on. They never learn anything, just as they never forget anything, though they do need to be reminded when someone is calling in a favour.

No one would describe them as particularly intelligent. They're certainly not intellectual. You never hear of a god or goddess reading, say, or having a conversation about the meaning of immortal life, though perhaps that's because immortal life has no real meaning. If you're immortal, nothing much matters because nothing is at stake. If they've got any sense, they steer clear of the theatre. Both the tragic and the comic playwrights tend to depict the gods in a negative light. Euripides represents them as calculating, vengeful and indifferent; Aristophanes as buffoons.

They have a knack for forming highly inappropriate relationships, often with humans. Most of these relationships end badly, particularly for the humans. Infidelity, one might say, is the norm rather than the exception. The pursuit of pleasure and honour pretty much sums up the purpose of their existence. What else is there for them to strive for?

Two of the things they like a lot are sacrifices and festivals. They also like receiving presents; the bigger, the more extravagant and the more plentiful the better.

Frightening they certainly are, but little reverence attaches to them. You can laugh at them and mock them to your heart's content, but just don't try to set yourself up as their equal. That's a recipe for disaster because they're extremely jealous. They're not only jealous of each other but also of humans, especially of anyone who's successful or accomplished. A number of myths show us how angry a god becomes if a human makes the claim that she or he is more accomplished in some skill or other. I can't say this too strongly: it's vital you keep on the right side of them. They'd be absurd because of their insecurity, if they weren't so bloody powerful.

We call them 'Olympians' because they inhabit Mount Olympus in northern Greece. Like the current members of the House of Windsor, they constitute a dynasty. The House of Zeus could at any moment be overthrown and replaced, which is what happened to its predecessor, the House of Cronus, and *its* predecessor the House of Uranus. This adds to their insecurity.

Not all divine beings live on Mount Olympus, however. There's also a subset that is subterranean. Subterranean deities – the technical term is 'chthonic', which means 'connected with the earth' – are associated with the dark forces that impact upon human life. Among them are the Furies, the Dread Sisters: viz. ugly crones who pursue and torment someone who has murdered a member of their own family. Another subterranean deity is Hecate, a goddess who uses the black powers associated with the dead to achieve her own dark ends. The dead, particularly the murdered dead, are vengeful and you can summon their support when you want to do harm to your enemy. The Greeks didn't build temples to the chthonic deities. Instead they worshipped them in caves, especially those with underground passages. We know much less about these infernal deities than we do about the Olympians, despite their prominence in myth, because they have left little trace of their existence in the archaeological record.

The other group who will be addressing you are the heroes. Heroes were once human but have been elevated to a higher status. Some of them are the product of a union between a human and a divine parent. A notable example is Achilles, the greatest warrior fighting on the Greek side in the Trojan War. Achilles' father, Peleus, was mortal and his mother, Thetis, was a sea nymph. Another example is Aeneas, the founder of the Roman race. His father was a mortal called Anchises and his mother was Aphrodite. They aren't saints. Far from it. They don't even have to be good people. Their lives may benefit humanity but that is not generally why they undertake challenges. Jason's quest for the golden fleece didn't serve any useful purpose. The golden fleece was simply *there* (rather like Everest is just *there* for mountaineers). Likewise, several of Heracles' twelve labours had no practical value.

Other individuals became heroes because of their exceptional experiences. Oedipus killed his father and married his mother. Orestes murdered his mother to avenge his father. Heroes have supernatural power, though when they die this power is limited to the area surrounding their grave. Their assistance can be summoned in time of need by blood sacrifice.

We shall also be encountering fate. Fate operates independently of the gods. It's an objective entity without any personality and, seemingly, without any agenda. It certainly acts without explanation. To discover what fate has in store for you, you can visit one of the many oracles scattered throughout the Greek world – the most famous of which is the Delphic Oracle, which is housed in Apollo's sanctuary – though you may not get a straightforward answer to your question. The gods are as much subject to fate as we are. Not surprisingly, the Greeks, despite being frightfully clever, never worked out the precise relationship between divine intervention, fate, and human freewill. That's because there *is* no precise relationship.

The Greeks believed that the divine and human worlds are interrelated, and it's for that reason that gods and humans sometimes enjoy a close, even intimate relationship. The most striking example is the bond that exists between Athena and Odysseus in the *Odyssey*. It derives primarily from the fact that they are both very cunning and take pleasure in hoodwinking their opponents. More often than not, however, these asymmetrical relationships come at a very high price for the human concerned. Hippolytus, who devotes himself exclusively to the worship of the virgin goddess Artemis, is destroyed by her jealous counterpart Aphrodite, goddess of love and female beauty, because she's incensed by the fact that he ignores her. Many myths, too, warn of the danger of hubris, exaggerated pride or self-confidence on the part of some human. Hubris invariably leads to nemesis, punishment or retribution.

Though gods and goddesses have their personal favourites, they aren't concerned with the welfare of the human race in general. Why should they be? What have they got to gain? Only exceptionally have the immortals shown any compassion or concern for us. The Titan Prometheus gave us the gift of fire. The god Dionysus taught us how to make wine.

For the most part they don't give a damn about us humans. There's an instructive moment in Homer's *Iliad* when Apollo says to Poseidon, 'Earthshaker' – that's the name for the god of the sea and of earthquakes – 'I would be bonkers to fight with you for the sake of mere mortals ... Let's abandon this quarrel and leave them to fight their own battles.'

Morally speaking, the gods would benefit by taking a leaf out of our book. There's a moment at the end of Euripides' *Bacchae* when Cadmus, Dionysus' grandfather, pleads with his grandson to show forgiveness. 'We implore you to spare us,' Cadmus says. 'We know we've done wrong.' 'I'm a god and you blasphemed me,' Dionysus replies. 'Gods should refrain from displaying human passion,' Cadmus observes. 'Zeus, who is my father, agreed to this long ago,' is Dionysus' casual rebuttal.

It's a chilling exchange. This is how the gods behave towards us most of the time; with utter indifference.

What is mythology? I'm not too keen on the hackneyed description of it as 'a storehouse of wisdom'. Of course, everyone is entitled to her or his definition of mythology, just as everyone is entitled to her or his interpretation of any given myth. Any myth is open to widely varying interpretations. That's one of the reasons why I would never arrange myths under headings such as 'myths of self-discovery', 'folkloric myths', 'myths explaining physical phenomena', and the like. A myth may do any of those things and much more besides. Mythology – here's my definition – provides a language for exploring the meaning of life and the terms of human existence without reference to some transcendent power or overarching plan. I challenge anyone to suggest there is any literary genre that does the job more successfully, given the fact that some of the most original thinkers have used it to illuminate our understanding.

Greek myths express the patterns that underlie human experience. They don't determine the consequences of those patterns. That's up to you and me. That's because they're so fluid and admit any number of variants in line with a profound, albeit somewhat contradictory, belief in freewill. Myths establish certain parameters within which repetitive cycles occur. They mostly exist outside time. If we try to establish some sort of chronological framework linking them together, major inconsistencies emerge. The Greeks didn't think of their myths as a logical or coherent body of literature.

Mythology is the product of a culture that transmits knowledge orally. Once that culture becomes literate, it either dies or assumes a different role. That is what happened in Greece. When literacy emerged, other ways of interpreting the world came into vogue and philosophical thinking was born. This is a gross simplification of a complex process, but not wildly inaccurate. The existing myths didn't die, however. They got retold and reinterpreted again and again, and with any luck will be retold and reinterpreted till the ending of the world.

Like anyone who writes a book on Greek mythology, I'm telling the stories in my own way. That's exactly what Greeks such as Homer, Hesiod and the rest did before me. That the myths continue to resonate today is due to the fact that, buried in their depths, lie truths about the world we inhabit, about human nature, and about our relationship with the divine. This remains true no matter how idiosyncratic the spin we put on them. It is because myths are so adaptable that they have lasted so long.

Though myths are highly adaptable, there are fixed elements in each. An oracle has decreed that baby Oedipus will grow up to kill his father and marry his mother. In Homer's version, Oedipus carries on ruling in Thebes when he discovers he has fulfilled the oracle, whereas in the version that Sophocles gives us in his play *Oedipus the King*, Oedipus blinds himself and goes into voluntary exile. The consequences of his unintended crimes and their discovery, however, are not fixed elements in the story. What matters profoundly and unalterably is the fact that Oedipus does not know that the man whom he kills is his father and that the woman whom he marries is his mother. He *has* to fulfil the awful prophecy and he *has* to come to a realisation of what he has done afterwards. But how you tell the story beyond that is up to Homer, Sophocles and you.

Oedipus wasn't afflicted with an Oedipus Complex, as Freud would have us believe, by the way. The theory assumes that a boy knows that the woman he is sexually drawn to is his mother, whereas Oedipus doesn't. What the Greek myth explores is human ignorance. It loses its meaning if Oedipus knows the identity of his biological parents. Hold on a minute, though. Who's to say that there doesn't lurk at the dark hidden core of this terrifying myth the suggestion that some sons *do* feel attraction towards their mothers and hostility towards their fathers? Greek myths are the common property of the human race, including psychoanalysts and psychopathologists. Freud, so to speak, invented a new myth.

Most myths predate the invention of writing. We have no idea how any of them came into being or was invented, who was its author, or how it was initially preserved. I assume that most of them predate writing and were recited over the fire at night by gifted storytellers, and that over time they travelled from one community to another and eventually entered the cultural Greek bloodstream.

Scholars often ponder the relationship between myth and history. While most myths are too far-fetched to have much if any basis in fact, a few clearly derive their inspiration from a historical event. The largest single body of myths involves the Trojan War, supposedly fought around 1250 BCE, which led to the destruction of Troy, a few miles off the northwest coast of modern-day Turkey, by a contingent of Greeks. Though the historicity of the Trojan War continues to be debated, most scholars concede that the tradition surrounding the war is based on a historical core.

Here's another fascinating question. Did the Greeks actually believe their myths? We could argue endlessly about that. They haven't left us much testimony on that score. The educated elite occasionally voice scepticism, but it is impossible to determine the majority viewpoint about the veracity of any given myth. What is clear is that the Greeks deemed their preservation essential.

There's no denying that some myths present a severe challenge to the modern sensibility. Take the myth of Procne and Tereus, king and queen of Thrace. When Procne's sister, Philomela, came for a visit, Tereus raped her. He then cut off her tongue and hid her in the forest so that she wouldn't be able to reveal his crime. However, the truth will out. When Procne discovered

Ajax carrying the dead body of Achilles from the battlefield.

what her husband had done, she murdered their son, Itys, and served him up to the unsuspecting Tereus in a casserole. There was no retribution for this terrible crime. Instead Procne was turned into a swallow, Philomela into a nightingale, and Tereus into a hoopoe. If you can find some profound meaning in this, other than the fact that people commit terrible crimes and their victims do terrible things in return, please tell me.

Incidentally, several motifs that we encounter in Greek mythology get rehashed time and time again. One is the 'serving-up-a-son-in-a-stew-to-his-unsuspecting-father'. Another is the 'failing-to-kill-an-infant-who-is-destined-to-kill-you'. These are the building blocks out of which many myths emerge.

This book comes therefore with a warning label. Its subject matter presents an exceedingly menacing and troubled landscape. Although myths don't entirely banish what is noble and generous in human nature, few of them have happy endings and many endings are frankly horrific, as in the case of the myth of Tereus and Procne. Such happiness as does occur tends to be purchased at the cost of much misery. I have found myself thinking constantly of the #MeToo movement. Violence against women is commonplace, more often than not involving a powerful male and a vulnerable female. However, the genre would cease to have its power to move and disturb if one were to eliminate the many instances of rape, homosexual as well as heterosexual, that occur, or in some other way try to sanitise it. In Ovid's epic poem *Metamorphoses* over fifty rapes occur. For that reason I haven't shied away from the nastiness.

Rape isn't the whole of it, however. We also encounter incest, infanticide, parricide, matricide, cannibalism – both the cooked variety and the raw – you name it, you'll find it here. Another day, another horror: that's the general message. Through Greek mythology we encounter the dark side of human nature, from which many of us would understandably prefer to avert our gaze. Yet it also provides us with an incomparably rich language for coming to terms with that dark side.

Greek mythology is very much alive and well in the contemporary world. There are many excellent narrative versions of the myths currently available, so I've tried to do something different here. I've adopted the technique of giving the characters the chance to tell their stories in their own words. This means that both gods and humans have the opportunity to reflect upon their fate. Well, fate isn't quite the right word. What I mean is that they have the opportunity to reflect upon their life stories and, in places, to justify their actions. In this way – I hope – they come across as flesh and blood people: or flesh and ichor people, in the case of the gods, ichor being the liquid that runs through their veins.

We're very lucky that the Greeks are still with us, and mythology is one of their greatest bequests. I'm not sure that we're capable of mythological thinking today. I'd be hard put to identify what we might call a modern myth in the sense in which I've been using the word here. The *Star Wars* cycle comes some way to achieving mythic status, but the cycle draws from well-established cultural mythemes without contributing much that is original.

When Ovid composed his *Metamorphoses*, he inventively connected myths by invoking the theme of shape-shifting, which enabled him to weave them together into a giant literary tapestry. I've attempted to link stories together by summoning a mythological character at the end of one story, who becomes the narrator in the next.

So here, without further ado, are the gods and heroes, in their own words.

Gaia

I'm old Earth, the primordial mother of every living creature. I'm way, way older than the Olympian gods. I give and I give and I give. In times gone by I gave without being asked. That was when I was inexhaustibly fertile. But those days are long since gone. I'm getting more and more worn out by the day. Producing is becoming too much for me. The bread-eaters have to scour my surface with their iron ploughs merely to scratch a living. Serves them bloody well right. That's why they call the present time the Age of Iron. If the bread-eaters don't show more respect to me, I'll stop producing altogether.

I haven't existed forever. Originally there was only Chaos. 'Chaos' in Greek doesn't mean the same as 'chaos' in English. It means 'Gaping Void' or 'Emptiness'. The Gaping Void gave birth to me without intercourse. Well, what else could it do? It also gave birth to Eros and Tartarus. You know what Eros is. Tartarus is the deepest and most forbidding part of Hades. We're a trinity: Earth, Love and Tartarus.

The bread-eaters describe me as 'ample-breasted'. Apart from my swelling contours, I'm just a flat disc surrounded by the encircling river Oceanus. Oceanus is my first-born. I had him with Uranus. He marks the limit of what the bread-eaters call the inhabited world. There's no life beyond his reach. Once you cross Oceanus, you come to Hades. That's where the dead live or more accurately where they exist. Helios, the sun, rises beyond Oceanus' eastern shoreline and sets beyond his western shoreline. He's married to Tethys. Oceanus' and Tethys' children – a cool 3,000 at the last count – are known as the Oceanids.

I don't have a head or arms or legs. None of the pre-Olympian deities do. The only body part I have, in addition to my ample contours, is a navel. When my son, Zeus, wanted to find out where my navel was, he released two eagles from Mount Olympus. They flew off in opposite directions and met at the Shining Rocks above Delphi, where Apollo's

1

oracle is situated. A navel is shaped like a maze, as you'll see if you take a look at yours right now. Navel-gazing gets a bad rap but it's not a bad thing. Like any navel, mine is all twisted up, but once you work your way through to the centre, you'll find the source of all wisdom. That's why bread-eaters make pilgrimages to Delphi: to get a handle on life's problems and discover insights about the future.

When I was first created, I was teeming with fecundity. I was so fecund that I didn't need a male to get me pregnant. Gender didn't exist. It was an afterthought, so to speak. I got on with the job and impregnated myself. That was how I gave birth to my son, Uranus, the Sky; just like Chaos impregnating him/her/itself and giving birth to me.

Uranus was also my first partner. If I hadn't mated with him, I'd have remained childless thereafter. He favoured the missionary position, which was fine by me, as I had no desire to lie on top of the sky. I and Uranus produced the Titans, six boys and six girls, who, likewise for lack of choice, mated with each other. They number – among other certain lesser-known entities – Oceanus, whom I've mentioned, Cronus, who in time (his name means 'Time') supplanted Uranus, Hyperion, the father of Helios, Mnemosyne, the mother of the Muses, Prometheus, the fire-stealer, Rhea, the wife of Cronus, Themis, divine law, and Tethys, goddess of the sea.

Uranus turned out to be the archetypal dysfunctional partner and father. He was so paranoid that one of his offspring would try to supplant him that he never gave me a moment's peace. Every time I gave birth, he would tear the poor, helpless little creature from my breast and hurl it down into the depths of Tartarus. What mother could endure that? Certainly not the mother of all mothers.

I therefore descended to Tartarus, unlocked the bronze doors, and released all my children. Then I fashioned a giant sickle with a jagged blade made out of gleaming adamant. Adamant is the hardest stone in the world. It's like diamond but even harder. I lined up all the Titans and asked which of them had the balls to castrate their father. Cronus, the youngest, eagerly volunteered. He's your archetypical alpha male.

That night the twelve all hid in our bedroom behind the curtains, scarcely daring to breathe. When Uranus was just about to descend on me as per usual, they sprang forth, grabbed hold of his limbs, and pinned him down. With one blow of his sickle Cronus severed his father's penis and tossed it into the sea.

'Now you're right royally bollocksed!' he cried exultantly,

Uranus let out a howl of agony. His blood burst out in thick dark gobs, splattering the walls and drenching me. I always say that you don't want to let a good thing go to waste, so I used the blood to create two new races: the Giants and the Furies. The Giants are, well, giants. Their bodies end in tails and they're pretty stupid. The fiercest are the Hecatoncheires, who have one hundred arms and fifty heads. The Furies are hideous females. They're pitiless avengers of the dead, especially of those who have been murdered by their family members.

Having cannonballed into the sea at great speed, Uranus' genitals were instantly transformed into shiny white foam, out of which sprang, fully grown, Aphrodite, the goddess of love and beauty. The name 'Aphrodite' derives in fact from the word *aphros*, meaning 'foam'.

Aphrodite first disembarked on Cythera, an island off the southern tip of the Peloponnese. There she boarded a waiting seashell and sailed to Cyprus, where she stunned the local population, who had never seen a goddess before, let alone one who had boarded a seashell. That's why Cythera and Cyprus are the foremost sites of her worship.

Aphrodite.

She's therefore the oldest of the Olympians, older even than Zeus, although you wouldn't think so to look at her. Uranus still lies on top of me, but now that he doesn't have a penis to flaunt, it's a pretty pointless exercise, which suits me down to the ground, literally and metaphorically speaking.

I also gave birth to Erichthonius, an early king of Athens, though not by Uranus. I became pregnant with him in a very curious way. Athena had visited the metal-working god, Hephaestus, to ask him to make some weapons and armour. While pretending to take her measurements, he grabbed hold of her by the waist. He quickly became aroused and tried to rape her, but the grey-eyed goddess shoved him off, with the result that he ended up ejaculating on her thigh. Athena wiped away his semen with a rag, which she tossed onto the earth, viz. onto me.

When baby Erichthonius came out of the earth, Athena, who saw herself as a kind of surrogate mother, hid the little fellow in a chest. She then presented the chest to the three daughters of King Cecrops, Athens' first king, with strict instructions not to open it. Well, of course they *did* open it. When they saw Erichthonius with a snake coiled around him, they were so horrified that they threw themselves off the Acropolis, which is where the palace was. The Acropolis is the rock that dominates the skyline of Athens.

Once Cronus had ascended to the throne, he was equally paranoid at the prospect of being ousted by his brothers and sisters. He therefore packed them all off down to Tartarus a second time. The one sibling he didn't send to Tartarus was Rhea, whom he married.

Immediately after he had slept with Rhea for the first time, Cronus received an ominous prophecy that one of his children would overthrow him. He became desperate. He couldn't refrain from sexual intercourse – that wasn't on the cards as an option – so there was only one course available. He had to get rid of his children. He came up with a particularly nasty plan. Every time Rhea gave birth, which she did with clock-like precision, he grabbed hold of the infant, popped it into his maw, and gulped it down with a swig of wine. After five of her children had met this fate, Rhea had had enough. So we came up with a plan. The sod didn't bother to chew, he just swallowed each infant whole, so as soon as Rhea gave birth to baby Zeus, we whisked him away and handed Cronus a stone wrapped in swaddling bands.

'Thanks, that'll do nicely,' Cronus said, popping the stone into his mouth and gobbling it down in no time flat.

Zeus was then reared on Mount Ida on the island of Crete on a diet of honey and milk by a nymph called Amalthea. She hid him in a tree so that Cronus, who had worked out that he'd swallowed a stone and was searching for him everywhere, wouldn't find him in heaven, on earth, or in the sky. To muffle his cries, a group of young men called the Curetes shouted and beat their spears against their shields, pretending to be performing a religious ritual so that Cronus wouldn't suspect that a lusty babe with superhuman lungs was being nursed on Mount Ida.

You're probably eager to hear about how the bread-eaters, aka the human race, came into being. Like the Olympians gods, they haven't existed forever. They've gone through several iterations. The first lot were made by Cronus. This was the Race of Gold. They lived like gods. I was so fertile in those days that they didn't have to work for their food. They didn't experience any sorrow or pain either. Every night they feasted and drank to their hearts' content. When they were ready to die, they fell painlessly asleep and I gathered them into my bosom. As a matter of fact they still wander at night around the earth. Bread-eaters evoke them when they need help. However, the Race of Gold were extremely arrogant. They refused to perform sacrifices to the gods, so Cronus annihilated them.

Since time immemorial every generation has always hoped that the next one will learn from the mistakes of its predecessor. It's never turned out to be the case in my experience, and I've seen a few generations in my time.

Anyway, back to Zeus. When he grew up, he went to his father's palace, determined to overthrow him. 'Who the Hell are you?' Cronus asked when Zeus marched into his palace one day in early autumn. 'I'm your long undigested son,' Zeus replied, slapping his father on the back four times. Each time he did so, one of his siblings popped out. They did so in reverse order to their birth, the latest born first.

Cronus didn't take his dethroning lying down, however. 'OK, all you Giants, stand up straight. We're going to wage war on Zeus. You Titans over there, come on, I'm enlisting you as well. Where do you think you're going, Themis and Prometheus?' 'Sod off,' said Themis and Prometheus jointly. 'We're joining Zeus.'

On Zeus' side were Demeter, goddess of the ripening corn and the harvest, Hades, god of the underworld and the dead, Hera, goddess of marriage and protector of wives, and Poseidon, god of the sea and maker of streams.

What followed is known as the Gigantomachy, or War of the Giants. It was hard fought. The turning point was a contest between Zeus on the one hand and Cronus' most powerful ally, a terrifying dragon called Typhoeus, on the other. Zeus was triumphant and the Olympians were finally victorious. As punishment for their insolence, Zeus stuffed the Giants inside the earth, i.e. me. It's very claustrophobic inside my guts and they're constantly squabbling, and this, in case you don't know, is the explanation of volcanoes.

Zeus hasn't faced any challenge to his authority since the Gigantomachy. Maybe he will one day. You never know what's around the corner in this world.

Zeus

I'm the most important and powerful of the Olympian gods. My official title is 'father of gods and men'. After I had overthrown Cronus, I drew lots with my brothers, Poseidon and Hades, to distribute our father's erstwhile powers. That's how I won control of the upper air and earth. Poseidon became lord of the sea lanes and Hades became lord of the underworld.

I'm a handsome fellow, though I say so myself. Well, I should be, shouldn't I, to be top god? Who wants to worship an ugly god? I'm in my forties. Well, actually I'm in my fifties, but as we all know, fifty is the new forty. Either way, I'm what you might call in athletic middle age. My hair is silvery grey and I wear it down to the nape of the neck, where it curls. My wife, Hera, is always saying that I'm constantly having a midlife crisis, which is why I'm always chasing after girls. The fact is I'm the divine embodiment of charismatic machismo. If anyone's having a midlife crisis, it's poor old Hera.

After my mother had enfolded the Race of Gold into her bosom, I decided to have a go at fashioning mortals, so I created the Race of Silver. I made some changes, however. No longer was it springtime all the year round. Instead there were four seasons. As a result, life was a lot harder. Mortals had to plant grain and seek shelter from the elements.

Zeus.

There was, however, a design fault in the make-up of this race, too. Their childhood lasted a hundred years and death occurred soon after. So, after a lot of humming and hawing I killed them all off.

Next I made the Race of Bronze, fashioned out of ash trees, which is what they used to make their spears. Their weapons, armour, cauldrons, and even their houses were made of bronze. They turned out to be even worse than the Race of Silver, however. The only thing they wanted to do all day was to kill each another and then eat one another's hearts out: literally. I concluded that annihilation was the only answer. I elicited help from Poseidon to flood the earth.

Out of the infinite bountifulness of my heart I spared two members of the Race of Bronze. This was a married couple called Deucalion and Pyrrha. Before Poseidon started flooding the earth, Prometheus advised them to construct a boat or an 'ark' as he called it. The sea level started rising and soon the whole earth was underwater. After they had been afloat for nine days, their ark finally came to rest on Mount Parnassus. When they saw all the bloated bodies of the people who had been drowned, Deucalion and Pyrrha were devastated. They became so desperate for human company that they asked the oracle of Themis at Delphi what they should do.

Themis told them to toss their mother's bones behind their shoulders. That was all. No explanation. They left her shrine in a state of total bewilderment. They had no idea what she meant.

'How can we be so disrespectful to our mother's bones?' asked Pyrrha.

They sat down and scratched their heads sorrowfully. Then Deucalion had a brainwave.

'Eureka! I've got it!' he exclaimed, leaping up. 'Our mother is the Earth and her bones are the stones!' he cried.

'Brilliant!' Pyrrha declared, leaping up in turn.

They hastened to the nearest field and began chucking all the stones they could find over their shoulders. Deucalion's stones became men and Pyrrha's stones became women. Soon the world had been repopulated. They called one of their sons Hellen. Hellen became the father of the Hellenic or Greek race. 'Greek' isn't a word the Greeks use of themselves. It's the name that the Romans assigned to them.

Like I said, Deucalion and Pyrrha were the very best of a bad lot and that's why I spared them. I drowned every other member of the Race of Bronze.

I now created the Race of Heroes. These were just as valiant as the Race of Bronze but more civilised. They honoured and respected the gods. This was the race that fought in the Trojan War. The greatest among them went to the Isles of the Blessed when they died. Admittedly there's not a lot to do in the Isles of the Blessed, but it does have a perfect climate. Most bread-eaters would give their eye teeth to live there, given the dreariness of Hades.

Currently it's members of the Age of Iron – viz. you lot reading this – who are populating the earth. It's called the Age of Iron because iron is the chief metal. I wouldn't want to be a bread-eater today. Their – your – life consists of endless toil and uninterrupted misery.

Achilles
brandishing
the head of the
Trojan Troilus.

There's so much evil and cruelty on earth that I've almost given up on the human race for the third time. However, if things are bad now, I predict they'll only get worse for you in the future. A time will come when babies will be born whose features resemble those of old men and women. That's when you'll know that the end of the world is nigh.

Some mortals think I'm emotionally shallow, but that simply isn't the case. I'm actually capable of very deep feelings. When my son, Sarpedon, was about to die at the hands of Patroclus, I was so upset that I wept floods of tears of blood. Blood is what the gods weep.

'I'm so upset,' I said to Hera. 'I don't think I can go on living.'

'Don't be ridiculous,' she replied haughtily. 'You don't have a choice.'

'Of course, I have a choice. I can bring him back from the dead.'

'Yes, you can do that in theory. But think what the consequences will be if you do.'

'All of us gods and goddesses have our favourites. If you start changing the rules about bread-eaters, we'll all follow suit and Hades will be up in arms.'

For once the old cow was right. So I told Apollo to go down to the battlefield to keep the flies away from Sarpedon's corpse, and I ordered Hypnos and Thanatos, Sleep and Death, to convey him back to his home in Lycia. In this way my son was spared the indignity of warriors fighting for possession of his corpse, which is what generally happens when a hero dies on the battlefield.

Despite the fact that I don't *always* do the right thing, I'm happy to report that there are some decent individuals who venerate me as the upholder of justice. One such was the Athenian playwright Aeschylus. Aeschylus went to great lengths in his trilogy of tragedies known as the *Oresteia* to prove that I reward good and punish evil, which at least sometimes is the case.

Between you and me, I'm not particularly concerned about what mortals get up to most of the time. Morality isn't my strong suit. The one thing I *do* care about *very much* is if a mortal swears an oath in my name and then breaks that oath. I think you call that 'taking my name in vain'. It's a bloody insult. I nuke any little sod who takes my name in vain with my thunderbolt. The thunderbolt is my special weapon. Keep this to yourself, but I'm a pretty poor shot. I often miss the offending bread-eater and blast a tree instead. Fortunately, mortals get the general point, and few of them risk swearing by me unless they're telling the truth.

Not long ago I descended to earth in the company of Hermes on a fact-finding mission. The world – again – was in a terrible state. Evil prevailed everywhere. One example out of many: Lycaon, the king of Arcadia, was too mean to sacrifice one of his prize oxen to me so he sacrificed his own son instead. That was the final straw. I turned the bugger into a wolf. He wasn't even fit to be a bread-eater.

I decided to see if I could find any mortals worth saving. After traipsing up and down the earth for months on end without finding a single candidate, Hermes and I finally arrived in Phrygia. It was a perfectly foul night. A violent storm was raging, overturning carts, uprooting trees, lashing mountains, flattening houses, and hurling pigs off cliffs. Wherever we went seeking shelter, however, mortals slammed their doors and sent us on our way. Eventually we came to a humble cottage with a thatched roof and wattle and daub walls. A solitary goat was tethered to a post in the yard.

I knocked on the door. An elderly man opened it. He invited us inside without a moment's hesitation. His wife took our wet cloaks, gave us dry clothing, and told us to make ourselves at home. It was as if they had been expecting us. They introduced themselves to us as Baucis and Philemon, husband and wife.

'We were just about to dine,' Baucis said, laying two extra places at the table. 'Please join us. We can offer you corn cakes, bean soup, honey, eggs and cheese. Everything comes from the little plot of land which we cultivate. Make yourselves at home.'

He offered us the only stools they owned and we sat down. The wine tasted awful, so while their backs were turned, I performed a miracle and – hey presto! – turned it into *grand cru*.

They both gave a start when they tasted the wine and realised we were no ordinary guests. I tipped the wink at Hermes and we shed our disguises. Baucis and Philemon fell to the ground, shielding their faces from the glare of our divine essence.

'Calm yourselves, dear hosts,' I said. 'We're not going to hurt you. This is Hermes and I'm Zeus.'

After we had eaten our fill and finished exchanging pleasantries, I decided it was time to flood the land and destroy all the miserable mortals who had rejected us. By the way, if this story is beginning to sound a bit familiar it's because I've flooded the earth twice.

I conducted the elderly couple up onto a mountain so that they would have a front row seat of the destruction I was about to hand out to the whole of humanity. I spared their house and their goat by making the waters swirl around their property without submerging it. I could tell they were impressed.

'You've been so hospitable that I'll grant you two wishes,' I said, slapping Baucis jovially on the back.

Husband and wife looked at each other. Then Baucis replied, 'Our first wish, father of gods and men, is to establish a cult in your honour and for us be its first priest and priestess.'

'*Rien de plus simple*,' I said loftily, slipping into a language they did not recognise, highly gratified. 'You got it. And the second wish?'

Again they exchanged glances. 'We'd like to die at the exact same moment,' Philemon said.

'I readily grant that too,' I said, bowing my head slightly, thereby causing a loud peel of thunder to drown out the sound of the torrential rain.

As an added bonus, when they died, I turned Baucis into an oak tree and Philemon into a lime tree. Their boughs began to entwine and they will forever be united.

You probably think it's a doddle being Zeus; all that power and no one to restrain you. Well, you'd be wrong. Most of the time being number one god is a pretty thankless job. I work hard and get so little thanks. I might remind you of the story of the sword of Damocles. Damocles was given to brown-nosing. He was always praising Dionysius, his king, for having such a blessed life.

'You think my life is blessed?' Dionysius said. 'How would you like to exchange places for one day?'

Damocles jumped at the suggestion. 'Do you mean it, sire?'

'I certainly do. You'll get to know exactly what it's like.'

'Wow!' said Damocles. 'My lucky day!'

Dionysius proceeded to attach a single horse's hair to the pommel of his sword and hang it above his throne. Then he ordered Damocles to take his seat on the throne. Warily the brown-noser did so.

'Now you know what it's like to live in fear that at any moment one of your enemies might stab you,' the king said.

Well, I'm immortal, of course, but the general point still holds. At any moment any god or Titan might try to supplant me and cast me down into Tartarus. Every dynasty has to be on guard.

My job does have *some* compensations, I'll admit. A lot of magnificent temples have been erected in my honour and I do receive some pretty sumptuous sacrifices. Oxen are my favourite, since you ask. Their savoury odour is to die for.

My best temple is in Olympia, the site of the Olympic Games. It contains a colossal statue of me seated on a throne. The statue is deemed one of the Seven Wonders of the World. It has a wooden core with ivory and gold placed on top. The sculptor, an Athenian named Phidias, was so gifted that you can almost see me breathing and perspiring. He's made me so big, however, that if I were to stand up inside the temple, my head would go through the roof. Outside is a huge mound of ash from all the oxen that have been sacrificed in my honour.

I suffer terribly from headaches as a result of all the hard work I do. On one occasion I had such a bad headache that I had to ask Hephaestus to relieve it. He raised his axe above his head and cut my skull open. Talk about a splitting headache!

The reason I was suffering from a headache was because – get this – my head was pregnant with the owl-eyed goddess Athena. The moment Hephaestus split my head open, Athena leaped out, fully grown, fully armed, brandishing her spear in warlike manner. All the gods were gobsmacked. The sun god, Helios, who as per usual was riding through the sky in his chariot, put the brakes on his chariot and brought it to a skidding halt, with the result that for a few moments time literally stood still.

Here's the back story. I'd impregnated a deity called Metis, whose name means 'Cunning' or 'Craftiness'. I'd received an oracle which said that any child to whom Metis gave birth would be wiser than its father. I obviously couldn't let that happen so, as soon as I ejaculated, I turned Metis into a fly and swallowed her. She and her foetus lived inside my head until Hephaestus split my skull. This meant that Metis wasn't actually Athena's mother. I was. Although Athena is a smarty-pants, she's certainly not smarter than me. You've got to think on your feet when you're in my position.

It's one thing to swallow a fly, quite another to swallow an infant. But that's exactly what my father Cronus did. Not just once but numerous times. After I had supplanted my father, I established the Olympian Dynasty. We're the third dynasty of gods to rule the earth. Probably my mother has told you all this already.

Another reason why my life is anything but a walk in the park is because I'm married to Hera. As top god, I think I have the right to indulge in unrestricted bonking, but the confounded woman is always spying on me. And does she know how to nag. Can you imagine being married to the same woman for all eternity? I mean, come on. I deserve a long service medal, if you ask me.

Divorce doesn't exist on Olympus. Besides which, I'm a man *dans la force d'âge*. I've played away from home with about one hundred women whose names I can remember, and hundreds, who's not to say thousands, whose names I can't remember. In my humble opinion humans as well as gods would both be a lot happier if we all stopped trying to be monogamous. It just doesn't suit our biological software.

I actually prefer liaisons with mortal women. Affairs with goddesses tend to land one in difficulties. The great thing about a relationship with a mortal woman is that it isn't going anywhere long-term because eventually she'll grow old and die. One-offs are my speciality. Inevitably all my relationships are what you lot call asymmetrical, but so what? Wouldn't you consider it an honour to experience my flattering attention? I'm hardly a frog.

Talking of frogs, I often turn myself into animals to avoid the prying eyes of Hera. To seduce a Phoenician girl called Europa, I disguised myself as a sleek white bull. One fine morning when Europa was out gathering bluebells – that's always the best time to make the moves on girls because their defence is down – she paused, looked up, and caught sight of me in a nearby field. She instantly became enamoured. I tossed my head back and forth, fixing my large brown eyes on her. It wasn't long before I had induced her to mount me. I then cantered over the sea to Crete, her legs astride me, in a manner of speaking, where, in the fullness of time, she gave birth to Minos, who later became king of that island. I immortalised our union by putting the constellation of Taurus, the bull, into the sky. Incidentally, Europa set something of a trend on the island. Minos' wife, Pasiphaë, also fell for a bull, as you will no doubt learn in due course.

I'm pretty solidly heterosexual, though there was one handsome lad whom I found rather fetching. His name was Ganymede. He used to pour my wine out at dinner. He was the son of Tros, the founder of Troy, though, like so many princes, he had been exposed at birth, discovered by shepherds, and raised as their own. He was tending his flock on

Zeus in the form of a bull, seducing Europa.

Mount Ida – not the Mount Ida in Crete but a different one – when I first took a shine to him. I disguised myself as an eagle, which wasn't difficult because that's the creature I'm most closely associated with, grabbed him by his shoulders by my talons, and wafted him up onto Olympus. I granted him eternal youth and generously gave his father some very fine horses.

Hera thought I was having an affair with the lad, which was a filthy lie. All the gods and goddesses found Ganymede hugely attractive. In the end, however, she gave me such a hard time that I had to banish him from Olympus. I set him in the sky as the constellation Aquarius, which means 'Water-carrier'. Check him out, so to speak, around the end of January.

Though mortals are my preference, I've had a number of affairs with goddesses. I've fathered loads of divine beings, including five Olympian deities: Hermes by the nymph Maia, Dionysus by the mortal Semele, Apollo and Artemis by the mortal Leto, and Athena by Metis.

My largest brood of offspring are the nine Muses, patrons of the arts. Their mother is Mnemosyne, or Memory. Makes sense, no? I mean if you want to be good at tragedy, or comedy, or history, or epic poetry, or lyric poetry, or sacred poetry, or astronomy, or dancing, you have to have a good memory. Homer evoked Calliope, the muse of epic poetry, at the beginning of the *Iliad* and the *Odyssey*. He couldn't have done what he did without her.

I also fathered the three Fates, the Moirai, by Themis, Divine Law. The Fates are old hags now because they've been around the block a few times. They determine the length of a mortal's life. Clotho does the spinning, Lachesis measures out the length of life, and Atropos snips the thread with her rusty scissors. Every mortal has a fixed number of years and there's nothing any of them can do to alter that sobering fact.

The only divine child I've ever had with my dear wife is the contentious, rancorous, argument-loving, grudgeful, lusty god of war, viz. Ares. Go figure. Ares is a tribute to the venom that characterises my relationship with Hera. Oh, I almost forgot. I also had Eileithyia with Hera. Eileithyia is the goddess to whom bread-eaters pray when they're experiencing birth pangs. She doesn't have much of a personality and I don't know of any temples that have been erected to her either. That's why I'm always forgetting her.

Hera once managed to become pregnant off her own bat, so to speak, i.e. by parthenogenesis. After infinite ferment she gave birth to Hephaestus. When she discovered the kid was lame, she tossed him out of Olympus without so much as a by your leave. He crash-landed on the island of Lemnos. Or maybe she threw him out of Olympus simply because she didn't like his looks and he only *became* lame when he landed on the island of Lemnos. That's why Hephaestus became a blacksmith. I mean, because he's lame. Blacksmiths don't need to be nimble on their pins.

I get on OK with my children. The most difficult to deal with is Artemis. That's because she hates sex. Don't ask me why.

Artemis

I refuse to have physical contact with men. It's against my religion. The thought of a man seeing me naked is utterly abhorrent. Once on a hot summer's day when I was taking a shower under a waterfall with some fellow-virgins, a huntsman called Actaeon inadvertently stumbled upon us. My companions all started screaming. I promptly turned him into a stag, whereupon he picked up his hoofs and galloped off. It was now his turn to be pursued by his hounds. They soon caught up with him and tore him limb from limb. I know what you're going to say. Actaeon wasn't actually *spying* on us. He was just at the wrong place at the wrong time. True, but I needed to teach voyeurs a lesson.

If I have any regrets, it's what I did to a sweet nymph called Callisto. Her name, appropriately, means 'Most Beautiful'. Callisto had no more interest in getting laid than I do. One morning, when the leaves were just beginning to turn in early autumn, my father, who bonks every girl in sight, observed her dressed in her huntswoman's outfit, i.e. bodice, leather skirt and high boots. He was immediately smitten and decided he must have her.

Zeus knew it wouldn't be easy, given the fact that Callisto was as hostile to sex as I am. He decided to gain her confidence by disguising himself as *me*. This was the cruellest of all his deceptions; turning himself into a goddess who is revolted by sexual intercourse in order to satisfy his insatiable sexual appetite.

Once he had gained Callisto's confidence by asking her all sorts of girlish questions like what sort of clothes she liked to wear, he invited her to sit down on a grassy bank. After a while he put his arm around her and began gently massaging her back. Pretty soon he became aroused. He did his best to conceal his erection, but Callisto spotted it and the game was up. She struggled to escape his clutches but resistance proved futile. He thrust her down onto the sward and, not to mince words,

Artemis.

had his way with her. After it was over Callisto gathered up her clothes and ran off. She was so ashamed that she never told a soul.

A few months later, when we were bathing together, I spotted her swollen belly.

'How dare you appear before me in that condition, Callisto!' I screamed. 'You've betrayed our sacred band. You're loathsome in my sight.'

Callisto burst into tears. 'Forgive me, divine mistress. I haven't betrayed you. I promise. It wasn't my fault. I tried to fight my assailant off but I couldn't prevent it. He was so much stronger. Please don't reject me!'

I refused to listen to her. Our law is quite clear on this point. It states that a girl is always at least partly responsible for her rape because she should have repulsed her assailant. I had no choice. Once you start making exceptions there'll be no end to the number of women who will try to get off the hook by using a similar excuse. It's my job to defend sexual mores, and if I don't do that, no one else will. I expelled Callisto from my sacred band. I confess I felt rather bad afterwards when I found out that it was my father who had raped her. A girl should be able to resist a man, but resisting a god is another matter altogether.

After I had expelled her, Callisto went off snivelling to Hera.

'What do you want?' Hera inquired testily.

'Your husband raped me.'

'Join the club,' Hera replied with a weary sigh. 'OK, I'll turn you into a woolly bear. That should cool his jets.'

A few months later Callisto gave birth to a boy called Arcas. Arcas grew up and became a hunter. One day he saw a bear slouching along on four paws. Not realising that the bear was his mother, he was about to shoot her when Zeus scooped her up. He set her in the sky as the constellation Ursa Major, the Big Bear. Arcas became Ursa Minor, the Little Bear. Mother and son will forever be united.

Because I'm the goddess of chastity, I protect young girls at puberty. They dedicate their toys in my sanctuaries, hoping to appease my anger before they engage in sexual intercourse.

You won't be surprised to know that I'm constantly at loggerheads with Aphrodite. Whereas I find sex dirty and degrading, Aphrodite can't get enough of it and wants everyone else to get as much of it as possible.

I don't understand it. Why should sex be the be-all and end-all of life? What's wrong with knitting a scarf?

She and I butted heads when a young man called Hippolytus, one of Theseus' sons, became fixated on me. I don't mean sexually fixated. Gods forbid. I just mean he worshipped me *exclusively*. He used to sing hymns to me all day long, praising the virtues of chastity. My kind of guy, in other words. Aphrodite fell into a jealous rage and planned her revenge. She wanted to teach all bread-eaters that if they fail to acknowledge their sexual urges, they're going to end up paying for it big time.

She caused Hippolytus' stepmother, Phaedra, to fall head over heels in love with him. Phaedra was the daughter of the Cretan king, Minos, and his ill-fated wife, Pasiphaë, who fell in love with a bull. You see where sexual desire leads you? Phaedra didn't know what had hit her. She became frantic with uncontrollable desire. She stopped eating, grew as thin as a rake, and moped about the palace all day. Her nurse knew something was up. Nurses always do. Eventually she managed to wheedle the truth out of her.

'What shall I do?' Phaedra demanded, after she had confessed her guilty secret. 'I can't carry on like this. I can't get the young man out of my head. I want to run my fingers through his thick hair. I want to stroke his puffy cheeks. I want to plant kisses on his ruby lips. I'm aching to touch his glistening skin.'

'Well, if that's what you want, mistress, there's only one thing you can do,' the nurse replied matter-of-factly. 'You're going to have to tell him the truth.'

This was exactly what Phaedra hoped to hear. However, for the sake of her honour, she pretended to be outraged.

'How can you suggest such a thing?' she protested. 'I wouldn't dream of telling him.'

The nurse shrugged nonchalantly. 'I don't see you have any alternative. You'll end up in the madhouse otherwise.'

'But what if he rejects me? He's never shown the least interest in me. Or in any other woman for that matter. I could be invisible as far as he's concerned.'

'That's because he's afraid to reveal his feelings to you,' the nurse said slyly. 'You're a very beautiful woman, Phaedra. Any young man would jump at the chance of going to bed with you. His inhibition is due to the fact that he's equally lovesick for you.'

'Do you think so? But what if people find out? I'll be so humiliated. And what about my husband? He'll kill me. He has a terrible temper.'

'Never mind about Theseus. He'll be none the wiser. He's away most of the time, getting up to gods know what. That's men for you. Just leave it up to me. I'll sort things out.'

'What are you going to do?' Phaedra asked apprehensively.

'Just put your mind to rest, dear,' the nurse replied, patting Phaedra's hand. 'The less you know the better. I have experience of situations like this.'

Less than an hour later Phaedra heard shouts coming from the garden. She looked out of the window and saw her stepson with her nurse. Hippolytus was stomping up and down.

'Tell your mistress she disgusts me!' he screamed. 'How could she think of such a disgusting thing, let alone confess it to you? As if I'd have an affair with my father's wife!'

Moments later he stormed into the palace to confront Phaedra directly.

'You should be ashamed of yourself. When my father returns, I'm going to tell him all about this. You're going to pay for this! He'll know what kind of slut he married!'

'Please don't,' Phaedra urged piteously. 'Forget what you've heard. I was out of my mind. I'll never embarrass you again.'

'Embarrass me!' he snorted. 'You think I care about that? It's your deceit that I can't deal with. Who knows how many men you've been unfaithful with! You revolt me!'

Phaedra retreated to her bedroom. She was mortified. It wasn't her fault, of course. Aphrodite had driven her to distraction.

She decided that only one course of action lay before her: to take her own life. She couldn't bear the thought of being remembered as a seductress, however. So she wrote a suicide note to Theseus, claiming that Hippolytus had tried to rape her. Then she tied a noose around her neck and hanged herself from a rafter in her bedroom.

When news of his wife's death reached Theseus, he was out slaying monsters. He immediately rushed home. As soon as he saw his wife's body slowly twisting from the rope, he was grief-stricken. Then he saw the suicide note. As he read it, he began shaking with rage. He immediately summoned his son. Hippolytus protested his innocence, but to no avail. His father cursed him in the name of his father, Poseidon.

'I never want to see your accursed face in this house again!' he shouted.

Traumatised, Hippolytus packed his bags and mounted his chariot. He flicked his whip and his horses set off at a trot along the shoreline. They hadn't gone more than a mile when a raging bull emerged from the sea. The horses took fright, reared up on their hind legs, and overturned the chariot. Hippolytus was tossed out and became entangled in the reins. His horses skittered about as they tried to avoid the bull, dragging his bloodied body over the jagged rocks.

A couple of slaves carried Hippolytus back home, his body a mass of cuts and bruises. Even now Theseus showed no sympathy. He was convinced Hippolytus had received just punishment for his terrible crime.

I couldn't stand aloof at such a moment. I sped down from Olympus and revealed to Theseus the full horror of what he had done, clearing Hippolytus of all guilt. I wish I could have arrived a few minutes earlier. If I had, the tragedy might have been averted. That's not how things work out, however. A curse is a curse. And besides, Aphrodite was determined to wreak havoc on the entire family. I've rarely seen her so angry.

There wasn't much I could do. Eventually I said, 'Look, I'm really sorry but I can't stay here any longer. You're just about to expire and it isn't appropriate for an Olympian deity to witness the exhalations of the dying. If I do, I'll become contaminated and you wouldn't want that, would you? I want to thank you most sincerely for your devotion to me over the years. You set a very good example to young men everywhere. They should all do as you did. I deeply regret that it has cost you your life. That, of course, is all due to that hateful b**** Aphrodite. But it was in a just cause. Your horrible death, I mean. Besides, I'll see to it that you haven't given up your life to chastity in vain. I'm going to establish a cult in your honour. Young men and women will forever evoke your name.'

What else could I tell the poor lad?

What *was* very moving was the touching scene of reconciliation that now took place between Theseus and Hippolytus. Theseus begged his son's forgiveness and Hippolytus readily accepted it. He didn't bear any resentment. Gods, as you know, are rarely capable of forgiveness. It's a human thing.

The only other man I've ever cared for was Orion.

Orion

The *mighty* hunter Orion, you mean, thank you very much. No hunter was mightier than I. After all, I'm the son of Poseidon. I'm also a constellation. I was transformed into a constellation by Zeus. You can see me up there with my dog, Sirius. His eye is the brightest star in the firmament.

Thanks to Poseidon, I had the ability to walk on water. No human had ever walked on water before. No human will ever do so again, of that I'm sure. I walked all the way to the island of Crete, skipping over the surf, the waves lapping at my heels. That was where I met Merope. On Crete, I mean. The girl dazzled me. I just couldn't resist her. She was the daughter of Oenopion, the local king. I blame Oenopion for what happened. He received me hospitably and kept plying me with drink. How could I say no? It wouldn't have been polite and I didn't want to offend. But the more I kept drinking, the more my inhibitions left me. I'd never tasted alcohol before.

I don't quite know the order of events from then on. It may have been the same night or it might have been the next day. Anyway, I got dragged before Oenopion. Merope was beside him, her dress torn. She was in floods of tears. She claimed I'd assaulted her. I denied it vehemently, but I had such a fearsome hangover that I wasn't able to mount a particularly effective defence.

After a brief interrogation, Oenopion called down a terrible curse on my head and, before I knew it, the lights went out. I was blinded. Far from being able to walk on water, I was reduced to groping my way around the solid earth. I was despised by all.

I could have ended my days as a pitiful reject, crouching on some street corner, shaking my begging bowl. But that was not to be my destiny. I'm far too manly and important for that. Eventually Hephaestus took pity on me. He told one of his servants to conduct me to the place where the sun rises.

There I encountered Helios, who cured my blindness and restored my ability to walk on water.

I've always liked women. The love of my life was Artemis. I know you'll think that's incredible, given the fact that she is the upholder of maidenly virtue. It was her unavailability that turned me on. But it wasn't all one-sided. Artemis had a soft spot for me too.

Her twin brother Apollo tried to warn her off me. He said I wasn't worthy of her, but she wouldn't listen to him. One day he challenged her to an archery contest. Artemis is highly competitive, so she immediately agreed.

Apollo took her down to the coast and pointed out an object that was bobbing up and down in the water.

'Bet you can't hit that,' he said teasingly.

'Bet you I can,' Artemis replied, smiling.

Artemis picked up her bow, drew back the string, took careful aim, and released the arrow. Bull's eye!

The only problem was that it wasn't any old object. It happened to be my head. I'd been innocently floating on my back at the time, interfering with no one.

Still, one has to look on the bright side. It was a pretty painless way to bow out (if you'll pardon the pun). I'd p***ed off Gaia by claiming that I was going to kill every living creature on the face of the earth – her face, that is – and she'd been manufacturing a scorpion that was going to sting me in the heel. I think the bow and arrow treatment was preferable.

Of course, Artemis was devastated, but a fat lot of good that did. So that's how Zeus converted me into a constellation by way of consolation.

All Apollo ever did was to make grief for his sister.

Apollo

I'm the god of reason, prophecy, rationality, plague, healing and music. When our mother, Leto, was pregnant, she had to wander all over the earth looking for a place to give birth. Nowhere would receive her. It was shameful. Eventually, just as her waters burst, she staggered onto the tiny island of Delos in the centre of the Cyclades, the 'Encircling Islands', so named because they surround it. Delos was only too happy to provide hospitality. The island thus achieved the distinction of being the birthplace of the divine twins.

Leto was in labour for nine days. The birthing goddess Eileithyia was constantly at her side. She didn't want to give birth in bed or even on a birthing stool (a stool with a hole in the centre so the baby can pop out). Instead she leaned against a tree, her legs outstretched. My sister emerged first. She was so precocious that as soon as Eileithyia had cut the umbilical cord she started assisting mother in her labours – in her remaining labour, I mean – which was giving birth to me.

I was no less precocious than Artemis. No sooner was I born than I picked up a bow and arrow that I saw lying on the ground and began target practice with some pelicans that were flying by. I also announced that I was going to be *the* chief god of prophecy. All the vegetation on the island burst into life in recognition of my unique talents. It hadn't taken me long to get all my ducks in a row.

One evening, when I was entertaining my sister with the lyre – at which I'm super adept – our mother came to us in floods of tears.

'What's the matter, mummy?' we asked in unison.

'I've been insulted by Niobe, the queen of Thebes. She's going around boasting that she's superior to me because she has seven sons and seven daughters, whereas I've only got you two.'

'Leave it to us,' we responded, again in unison.

We immediately sped to Thebes. Within minutes I had shot and killed all seven of Niobe's sons. My sister had shot six of her daughters. She was taking aim at the seventh when Niobe fell on her knees and begged her to spare the last one. All to no avail. My sister took careful aim and shot her through the heart.

Niobe buried her head in her hands. She couldn't stop crying. She cried for days on end. No one could console her. Eventually her tears began to harden in the sun and turned into amber. That's why amber appears to weep tears.

My principal sanctuary is at Delphi, the foremost seat of oracular pronouncements. Delphi was previously under the jurisdiction of Gaia, but I killed the python that was guarding her sanctuary.

Like I said, I'm the god of music. My half-sister Athena invented the flute. When she tried to play it, however, her cheeks puffed up and she thought this made her look ugly, so she threw the instrument away in disgust. I picked it up and became a divine flautist.

One day an insolent satyr called Marsyas challenged me to a competition.

'I bet I'm a better flautist than you,' he said with a smirk.

'What if you lose?' I asked.

'I'll submit to any punishment you like,' he replied, smirking a second time.

I summoned the Muses as judges and we held a contest. Marsyas whipped the Muses up into a frenzy, whereas I transported them to an unearthly realm. The Muses declared me the winner.

By way of punishment I hung Marsyas upside down from a tall pine tree. Then I flayed him alive, cutting the strips of flesh from his body with painstaking care. He was still smirking. I rather fancy he thought he had actually played better. Bloody satyr.

Another insolent individual was a girl called Arachne. Arachne was a fantastic spinner. Her fingers could weave the most amazing images within the twinkling of an eye. Athena, who excels at spinning herself, told her to desist. When she refused, Athena challenged her to a weaving contest.

Athena wove a tapestry that depicted the gods behaving nobly, whereas Arachne depicted them indulging in rape and other deplorable activities. Athena was so angry that she struck Arachne with the back of her hand, causing a huge angry welt to swell up on her cheek. Arachne felt so humiliated that she hanged herself.

'Since you like spinning so much,' Athena said to her, 'you can go on spinning forever.' Whereupon she transformed her into a long-legged spider.

I'm an incredible lover, even though many of my affairs haven't turned out quite the way I would have wanted. Keep this to yourself, but I've been rejected more times than I care to remember. I don't understand it. What girl wouldn't be thrilled to be ravished by a god, especially a youthful god with flaxen hair, broad shoulders, narrow hips, and endowed with the full nine yards, metaphorically speaking?

Well, quite a few, it seems. Take that nymph Daphne for starters. I was about to enfold the girl in my passionate embrace when the little cow offered up a prayer to some river god, who promptly turned her into a laurel tree. Before I knew it, instead of sinking my nails into her enticingly plump flesh, I was rubbing up against the hard, knobby bark of a laurel tree.

'Even though you have rejected me, Daphne,' I said, stroking the leaves of the tree affectionately, 'I'll consecrate a wreathe in your memory. The laurel wreath will always symbolise my undying love for you.' *Très gallant*, no?

Another girl who rejected me was Ares' granddaughter, Marpessa. Marpessa had eloped with her lover Idas. When Marpessa's father found out, he was filled with shame and committed suicide. I caught sight of Marpessa one day while she was picking bluebells in a lush meadow and became filled with desire. I swooped down and snatched her up to Mount Olympus.

Zeus was furious. 'You can't just abduct any girl who takes your fancy and bring her up here. That's bending the rules. What makes you think she wants to live here? Have you asked her?'

The silly girl chose Idas. She said that I'd eventually tire of her. Well, I suppose I can't argue with that. Even so, we could have had a few good tumbles in the hay.

I was also very fond of a Spartan prince called Hyacinthus, though that didn't end well either. He and I used to get our kicks by hurling bronze discuses at one another and trying to catch them. Once I threw my discus so high into the sky that it vanished into the clouds.

Eventually it came spinning down to earth, making a terrific whirring sound. Hyacinthus ran forward to catch it, but he just missed it. The discus landed on the ground, bounced, and hit him full in the face. He died instantly. I tried to revive him with my medical arts – I'm god of medicine, remember – but he was as dead as a doornail. In his honour I caused a flower to spring up from the soil that had been soaked with his blood. That's how hyacinths were invented.

Talking about medical arts, I'm not only the god who causes plagues but also the god who brings relief from plagues. I caused a plague to attack the Greek army in the tenth year of the Trojan War. I did that because Agamemnon, commander-in-chief of the Greek army, was sleeping with a war bride called Chryseïs. She was the daughter of my priest, Chryses. He said it was an insult to my dignity as well as his, which it was. That's why I caused the plague. Only when Agamemnon gave the girl back did I call the plague off.

My son, Asclepius, took after me in excelling in the art of medicine. His mother was a ravishingly beautiful Thessalian princess called Coronis. This was another affair that went south. I had decided to ask Coronis to marry me when a raven appeared at my window one morning. In ravenspeak he told me he'd seen Coronis with another man.

I was so angry that I shot an arrow into Coronis' heart. She was carrying my child at the time, but my pride had been insulted.

'I swear by Zeus and Hades and all the immortal gods that I was never unfaithful to you,' Coronis exclaimed with her dying breath.

I realised too late that the raven had duped me. I rescued the foetus from her womb and cursed all ravens by turning their feathers as black as soot as a sign of their incorrigible mendacity. Previously their plumage had been white.

I placed Asclepius under the tutelage of the centaur Chiron. He became a gifted doctor but he went too far. When Hippolytus died, after being cursed by his father, Artemis asked him to resurrect him. Asclepius told her that there were limits to what he should do, but my sister wouldn't take no for an answer. So he caved in and brought Hippolytus back from the dead.

Hades created a terrible stink when he found himself deprived of one of his inhabitants. One day there was Hippolytus among the denizens of the Underworld and the next there he was walking around back on earth without a care in the world. Zeus was furious.

'You can't go around upsetting the natural order of things!' he boomed, causing the clouds to slam into each other. 'There's a place for the living and a place for the dead and ne'er the twain shall meet.'

And with that he struck Asclepius full in the chest with his thunderbolt, reducing him to a smoking pile of cinders. I was furious in turn: so furious that I killed all the Cyclopes who manufacture Zeus' thunderbolts. This just made matters worse.

'You insolent wretch!' Zeus boomed again, banging his fist on the arm of his throne, causing the entire earth to tremble. 'You can damn well be a slave for a year. That'll teach you a lesson.'

'A slave!' I protested. 'I can't be a slave. I'm a god. That's the ultimate insult.'

'You'll do as I say, boy. You need to learn how to behave yourself.'

Zeus packed me off to Thessaly to serve Admetus, the local king. Admetus turned out to be a likeable enough fellow and we got on as well as could be expected, given the fact that I, a god, was his slave. If *that* isn't upsetting the natural order of things, I don't know what is.

After I'd been serving him for about six months, Admetus summoned me into his study. I'd been polishing his hunting boots at the time. I'd never seen him looking so miserable.

'I need your advice,' he said. 'I've just had some rather bad news. I've been told I have only a short time to live. Can you think of any way to avert the inevitable?'

'I'm very sorry to hear that, Admetus,' I replied sympathetically. 'I'll see what I can do. I'll have a word with the Fates.'

'Thanks.'

'Don't mention it. It's the least I can do.'

After a lot of wrangling I finally got the Fates to agree to extend Admetus' life, but only on condition that he found someone to die in his place. A substitute cadaver, in other words.

'Who on earth can I ask?' Admetus demanded, scratching his beard, when I told him what the Fates had said.

'What about your parents?' I suggested.

'That's a great idea!' he replied enthusiastically. 'Why didn't I think of that? They're elderly anyway, and losing a year or so should be no big deal, especially if it means extending the life of their son.'

'Right you are,' I agreed. 'It won't be much skin off their noses, or the nose of whichever one volunteers.'

Admetus laughed at my joke. I was glad to have cheered him up.

Well, it turned out that it *was* a big deal because neither of his parents was prepared to make the sacrifice. They both claimed that human life wasn't any the less precious when it got closer to the end.

'It turns out that neither my mum nor my dad love me enough to die for me,' Admetus said sorrowfully to his young wife, Alcestis, that evening at supper, quite beside himself.

'I do,' Alcestis replied, casting her eyes downwards.

'You do?' he exclaimed. 'Really? I was beginning to think that no one loved me. I'll never forget this, Alcestis.'

'I'll take my ritual bath before I die to spare the slaves from having to bathe my corpse afterwards, as custom dictates,' Alcestis added obligingly.

'That's really thoughtful of you. I'm sure they'll appreciate that. Bathing a corpse is never a very pleasant task.'

Admetus was a very lucky man. I don't know any woman who would die for me, I'll say that. Not that the issue would come up since I'm a god.

Just as Alcestis was about to breathe her last, however, who should turn up at the house but that slovenly oaf Heracles. He was four sheets to the wind as usual. At first Admetus, acting the part of the consummate host, tried to keep his guest from knowing that he had come to a house of mourning. He didn't want to look inhospitable. But eventually Heracles twigged it. As ever, the hero was up for a challenge.

'Perhaps I can help you, Admetus,' he said.

'I don't see how,' Admetus replied. 'The Fates have insisted that someone dies in my place and this is the only offer I've had.'

'I'll sort things out,' Heracles said mysteriously.

Soon afterwards Thanatos – Death – arrived at the house to take Alcestis down to Hades. He found more than he was bargaining for, however. As soon as he stepped over the threshold, Heracles arm-wrestled him to the ground. Thanatos was no match for Heracles. He was forced to depart empty-handed with his metaphorical tail between his legs. So in the end Admetus and Alcestis lived happily ever after.

Or perhaps not. It's difficult to see how domestic harmony could ever have been established again.

Anyway, back to Asclepius and how he got struck with a thunderbolt for resurrecting Hippolytus. Many years later Zeus relented and allowed him to take his place among the gods up on Olympus. Henceforth, humans suffering from neuralgia, phlebitis, diabetic gangrene, sciatica, eczema, gout, dementia, stroke, anxiety, cellulitis, infertility, constipation, acne – I could go on and on – have had a god to pray to.

I epitomise the Greek spirit more than any other god, since I'm cultivated, athletic, artistic, rational, and so forth. It beats me why I don't get more respect or laid more often. The worst insult to my dignity came from Hermes. The little blighter tried to get the better of me the day he was born.

Hermes

I'm Hermes. I'm the son of Zeus and the nymph Maia. I'm the god of businessmen, bounders, boundaries, heralds, highway robbers, traders, thieves, trespassers, tricksters, cardsharps, cads, cheats, con-men, liars, lispers, loblollymen, losers … you name it, I've got a hand in every pie. I also carry messages to earth from Olympus on behalf of Zeus. You can recognise me by the fact that I wear a helmet and boots with little wings attached. These enable me to fly at the speed of light.

It was I who secured safe conduct for King Priam when he passed through the Greek lines to seek the return of his son's body from Achilles. It was I who gave Odysseus inside information about how to trick the witch Circe. It was I who bore the message to Calypso from Zeus ordering her to break off her relationship with Odysseus. I'm always flitting about between Olympus and Earth.

You don't need a pricey statue to worship me. Any old heap of stones will do. A heap of stones marks a boundary because I'm the god of boundaries, like I said. Sometimes you'll see me depicted in the form of a head on top of a column with an erect penis. An erect penis is the best thing there is at scaring away would-be thieves and trespassers. I'm not only the god *of* thieves, you see, but also the god who protects against thieves.

The moment I was born, it didn't take me long to find my feet. By midday I had invented the seven-stringed lyre. I made the sound box out of a tortoise shell. Then I cut up a piece of ox-hide to make the box resonate and used sheep gut for the strings.

I soon got bored with it and wanted a new challenge, so I decided to steal Apollo's cattle. I made them walk backwards so that their owner would go looking for them in the opposite direction. Tricky, no? I then returned to my cradle and pretended to be an innocent baby in whose mouth butter would not melt.

Eventually Apollo came across a shepherd who revealed what I'd done. He appeared before my mother and demanded reparations. She had no option but to lead him to me. I looked up at Apollo with my cute little eyes but he wasn't deceived. He snatched me out of my cradle and carried me, kicking and screaming, up onto Olympus. He then appealed to Zeus to adjudicate between us. I lied through my toothless gums. I even took a mighty oath – by Zeus no less – swearing that I had no knowledge of the theft. Then I turned my baby eyes on Zeus as well. At that, he could no longer keep a straight face and burst out laughing.

'Just return the cattle to Apollo,' Zeus said indulgently. 'And mind you behave yourself in the future, my boy. Otherwise, I'll … I'll just … you wait and see.'

Yeah, right, as the saying goes. I had no intention of behaving myself. Not for anyone. It's far more fun being bad.

Later that same day – this was all still the first day of my life – I sang to Apollo to the accompaniment of my lyre.

'You're pretty good at that,' he conceded.

'Thanks, would you like it?'

'The lyre you mean? Thanks. Here, I'll give you fifty of my cows in payment. You can be lord of all cattle from now on'.

Henceforth we've got on pretty well together, even though he's still sore from the trick I played on him.

Since I'm god of all sorts of miscreants, there are lots of lowlifes who take me for their god. One such was Procrustes, who terrorised travellers on the way from Athens to Eleusis. Procrustes ran a hostel. Whenever anyone passed by, he'd invite them to sleep in a nice comfy bed free of charge. If the guest was too tall for the bed – no problem – he would cut off the extra bit of their body so they would fit perfectly. If the guest was too short – no problem again – he would stretch them out. No one fitted perfectly so there was always some small adjustment to make. Procrustes amused himself by doing this for a number of years until Theseus put a stop to his little antics by fitting him to his own bed. Since he was far too tall, Theseus had to cut off both his legs and his head.

Another of my devotees was Sinis. He used to tie travellers between two tall pine trees by their arms and legs. He bent the trees to the ground so that the tension was extreme, and suddenly released them.

His victim was torn limb from limb. Theseus seized Sinis and gave him a taste of his own medicine. Then he kicked his dismembered trunk into the sea.

Yet another monster of depravity for whom I had a rather soft spot was a rogue called Sciron. Sciron used to block the path of travellers on a narrow dirt track that ran close to the edge of a cliff. He told them he would only let them pass if they stopped to wash his smelly feet. The rogue was huge, so no traveller could pass by without doing what he demanded. When his victim was scrubbing his feet energetically, Sciron kicked him off the cliff into the water, where a monster was waiting, its slavering jaws open. Theseus grabbed hold of the miscreant's foot and dragged him, screaming, over the cliff to be devoured by the sea monster in turn. The roads leading out of Athens have become a lot safer now that Theseus has cleared away so many obstacles.

Moving on to the subject of sex, the biggest love of my life was Aphrodite, whom I got pregnant. When Aphrodite gave birth, we couldn't decide what to name the child. Eventually we came up with the double-barrelled name 'Hermaphroditus' (get it?). This by the way is the origin of all double-barrelled names.

One day Hermaphroditus was out wandering when he came to a pool of clear water. Being entranced by its beauty, he paused at the edge to gather some flowers. It so happened that the pool was inhabited by a nymph called Salmacis, who swam to the surface and seated herself beside the youth, their shoulders touching. Salmacis was smitten. She placed her hand on his thigh. When she bent forward and placed her lips on his, however, he pushed her roughly away. The nymph blushed, apologised profusely and pretended to run off in shame. In actual fact, however, she hid behind a tree. To her delight, Hermaphroditus then stripped naked and dived into the water.

Salmacis dived in after him. She clasped him to her ardent breast and began planting kisses all over his naked body. At first, he writhed in an effort to shake himself free, but without success. The more he writhed, the tighter she clung. In the end, he, too, became aroused and gave himself up to the unearthly delights of underwater sex with a nubile nymph. Their bodies entwined and before long their flesh merged into one. No longer were they boy and girl. Henceforth they were girl-boy or boy-girl. There was no distinction. This is the origin of hermaphroditism, aptly named after the most playful of the gods (me!) and his stunningly beautiful mistress, Aphrodite.

There's one other job I perform. I'm also the *psychopompos,* the leader of souls, meaning I'm the god who conducts the dead down to the Underworld. When someone dies, I swoop down and tap their eyes with a short staff called a caduceus. This enables the dead to grope his or her way down to Hades along 'the mouldy way'. It's called 'mouldy' because it's littered with billions of little flecks of flesh that rub off the corpses as they make their way to their final resting place below earth.

I don't know how mortals face up to their mortality. It must be quite a challenge. Some of them die as soon as they're born. The gloomy playwright Sophocles said that dying as soon as you've been born is the next best thing to not being born at all.

Talking about birth, lots of heroes, like Perseus, have been at risk the moment they've been born because of a prophecy that they're going to do great or monstrous things.

Perseus

My grandfather Acrisius, the king of Argos, wanted to strangle me at birth. He'd received a prophecy that his grandson would kill him when he grew up. The only reason he didn't strangle me was because he knew that if he did, Zeus, who happened to be my father, would kill him.

Acrisius had imprisoned his daughter, Danaë, inside a bronze tower in order to prevent her from attracting the attention of any man. The tower was without any doors or windows. There was only a narrow skylight, but it was just large enough for a shower of golden rain to penetrate. Which is how Zeus impregnated Danaë. It was the only way he could gain access to her.

As soon as I was born, Acrisius seized me and my mother and nailed us inside a small wooden crate so that we could scarcely breathe. Then he told his servants to toss the chest into the sea. He was confident that the waves and the rocks would do the job that he feared to do himself.

Against all odds my mum and I survived, however. After being buffeted by the waves for days, we eventually washed ashore on a tiny island called Seriphos. It was ruled by a king called Polydectes.

I didn't care for Polydectes one bit. From the word go he started to put the moves on my mother, even though she made it perfectly clear that she wasn't interested. Years passed, I grew to manhood, and Polydectes decided his life would be a lot easier if he could get rid of me, as he saw me as an obstacle to his happiness.

One day, he announced that he was holding a feast. He informed all the guests, including me, that we were required to bring him a horse as a gift. Well, I didn't own a horse, so I asked him what else I could bring. I rashly promised to give him whatever he wanted.

'Actually I'd like you to bring me the head of the Gorgon Medusa,' the king pronounced, rubbing his hands gleefully.

I was, as they say, up the creek without a paddle. I'd agreed and there was no way I could get out of it. Gorgons are terrifying creatures.

The Gorgon Medusa.

There are – or were back then – three of them: two immortal ones, Stheno and Euryale, and one mortal one, Medusa. Gorgons have venomous snakes in their heads. They can turn you to stone if you look them in the eye, so it wasn't just a straightforward case of killing a monster. Any fool with a bit of brawn could have done that. Instead I had to avert my eyes while performing the deadly deed.

Fortunately, the goddess Athena came to my rescue. She told me to go to the Hesperides, the Daughters of Evening, and ask for some magic objects to help me kill Medusa. Reaching Hesperia presented another big challenge because no one knows exactly where it is, apart from the fact that it lies somewhere in the west where the sun sets. This meant that I also had to seek the help of the three Graeae, the Grey Ones, ugly old hags who actually knew its address.

The distinguishing feature about the Graeae is that they possess only one eye and one tooth between them. They were in the process of passing their single eye from one to another when I happened to turn up. I hastily snatched the oily ball from their claw-like fingers.

'Give it back! Give it back! Give it back!' each of them chirped in a gravelly voice.

'Not till you tell me how to get to Hesperia,' I replied resolutely.

'Oh, all right,' they agreed reluctantly.

Once the Graeae had told me where to go, I tossed their eye onto the ground and went on my way. I heard their fingers scratching the earth in search of it.

The Daughters of Evening turned out to be very helpful. 'You'll need a cap, so that you can sneak up on Medusa without her seeing you,' said one. 'Try this for size.'

'And a bag to put Medusa's head in, so that you don't see it after you've cut it off,' said another. 'You're welcome to borrow this one.'

'And a pair of winged sandals,' chirped in a third. 'See if these'll fit you. They're the ancient equivalent of booster rockets. It'll take you forever to reach the Gorgons unaided. They'll also help you to escape from her sisters, Stheno and Euryale. They're bound to give chase after you've killed Medusa.'

I thanked them profusely, attached the sandals to my feet, and sped off.

As soon as I reached the domain of the Gorgons, I tiptoed up behind Medusa and tapped her lightly on the shoulder. Instantly she spun around, but I held up my bronze shield, so she found herself staring at her own reflection. Carefully averting my eyes, I cut off her head, moments before it turned into stone.

This wasn't the end of my adventures, by any means. On my way back from the ends of the earth, I stopped off to see Atlas, who supports the world on his shoulders. I was feeling exhausted and needed some refreshment. The bugger refused to give me even a beaker of water, so I took Medusa's head out of the bag and pointed it at him. He turned to stone in the twinkling of an eye. That's how the Atlas Mountains came to be formed.

Later down the road I encountered an attractive blonde with corkscrew curls that tumbled all the way down to her waist. She was chained to a rock, guarded by a vicious-looking, fire-breathing dragon.

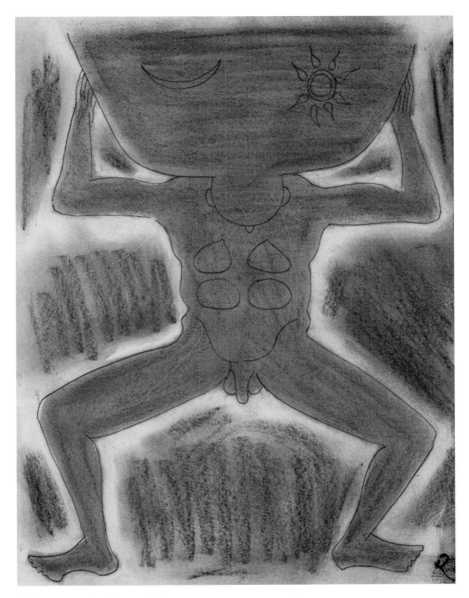

Atlas supporting the world.

'Hello, maiden. Are you by any chance in distress?' I inquired, tipping my cap.

'Indeed I am, sir,' the blonde replied. 'I'm stuck here because my mother, Cassiopeia, boasted that she was more beautiful than all the

Nereids. In case you don't know, they're the fifty daughters of Nereus, otherwise known as the Old Man of the Sea. Nereus sought revenge from Poseidon because of my mum's insolence, and Poseidon answered his prayer by imprisoning me on this rock. It's not fair. I've done nothing wrong. I'm being punished solely for my mother's insolence.'

'It's very unfair,' I agreed. 'What's your name by the way?'

'Andromeda.'

'Would you like me to dispose of the dragon, Andromeda?'

'Would you?'

'On one condition.'

'What's that?'

'That you agree to marry me.'

'I'm afraid I'm engaged already.'

'Who's the lucky man?'

'My uncle, Phineus, son of Belus.'

'Your uncle! Break it off.'

'How?'

'Leave it up to me.'

I held out the Gorgon's head to the fire-breathing dragon, whereupon the creature turned to sandstone and disintegrated. Then I sped off to Phineus' palace.

As soon as I arrived, I knocked on the door. It was opened by a tall, ruddy-faced man with giant biceps.

'Are you Phineus, son of Belus, by any chance?' I inquired.

'The same. And who might you be?'

'Here, get a butcher's at this,' I said. Then I whipped out Medusa's head from the bag and pointed it in his direction.

He instantly turned to stone. So that's how I married Andromeda.

When I returned home to Seriphos, I showed Medusa's head to that pesky fellow Polydectes, who was still itching to marry my mother, and he turned to stone as well. A handy little instrument, that head, I thought.

After I'd completed these exploits, I gave Medusa's head to Athena as a thank you offering for her help. She wears it on her breastplate. She calls it her Gorgoneion. It strikes fear into her enemies.

It was from the blood of Medusa that the winged horse Pegasus sprang.

Bellerophon

I loved Pegasus. He was an amazing creature. We had a very special bond. He'd been raised by the Muses. It was just his bad luck to get involved with me.

I've never had much luck. Take the day I proposed to that long-legged, creamy-skinned brunette called Aethra. She was the daughter of

The winged horse Pegasus.

Pittheus, king of Troezen. I had had the hots for her for months. So one day I decided to take the bull by the horns. I put on my best *chiton* and carefully combed my long hair. I took my brother, Alcimenes, along for moral support.

We climbed the hill to Pittheus' palace and knocked on the door. After a few minutes the door opened and we were shown into the throne room.

'All hail, Pittheus, son of Pelops!' I exclaimed, kneeling. 'I'm a hero and I've come to request the hand of your daughter in marriage.'

'A hero, you say?' the king said, impressed. 'What's your name?'

'My name is Bellerophon, and I'm the son of Poseidon.'

Pittheus rose from his chair and extended his hand, indicating that he was inviting me to abandon my semi-recumbent posture.

'Very well, young man,' he declared. 'My daughter's yours. Let's go and do a bit of target practice. It's a good way for males to bond and I need to stretch my legs.'

Alcimenes and I followed Pittheus out into the garden and we began throwing spears. Being a hero, I'm usually a pretty dab hand at this sort of thing and can hit a bull's eye at a thousand paces. But on this occasion my grip on the spear I was holding slipped just as I threw it. The spear veered off to the right and struck Alcimenes full in the chest. He fell to the ground, gasping his last, his blood staining the ground with a rapidly expanding pool.

'Oh, my gods!' I exclaimed, running forward and clasping his lifeless body. 'What on earth have I done?'

'You've just killed your brother, you blithering idiot,' Pittheus spluttered, seething with rage. 'And what's more, you've polluted my home. You're a hateful being, hateful to mortals and immortals alike. Get out immediately! Don't ever let me see your accursed face in Troezen ever again.'

I wandered the pathless ways shunned by all, an abhorred being, for months, perhaps years. I lost all sense of time. Then one day I arrived at the palace of Proetus, king of Tiryns, not far from Mycenae. Proetus, as it so happens, was my grandfather, Acrisius', twin brother. Small world.

'All hail, Proetus, son of Abas,' I said on one knee. 'I am Bellerophon, son of Poseidon. I've humbly come to seek expiation for a terrible crime. Your fame in performing expiations has reached the ends of the earth.'

'What exactly is your crime?' Proetus inquired, beckoning me to stand.

'I accidentally killed my brother.'

'Accidents will happen,' Proetus said comfortingly. 'I can't stand my brother. I'd kill him, given half the chance. I was entitled to half the kingdom of Argos but he drove me out. He also accused me of seducing his daughter, Danaë. Can you imagine? What kind of a person would do that?'

'Danaë? You mean the girl whom Zeus seduced in the form of a shower of golden rain?'

'The same. At least I think it was the same Danaë. It's a rather common name. Anyway, why don't you stay a few days? My wife and I would be delighted to entertain you. It gets rather dull in Tiryns in the winter. Wouldn't you agree, Sthenoboea?'

Proetus cast an adoring glance in the direction of the woman seated beside him. She had a sizeable cleavage, curly blonde hair, and deep blue eyes. She winked at me. I didn't know quite what to do, so I winked back.

'Thanks, Proetus,' I replied. 'That's a very generous offer.'

'What you need is pig's blood for purification,' he said, snapping his fingers.

A slave immediately materialised, as slaves do, from nowhere.

'Bring this young man a bowl of pig's blood,' he ordered. Then turning to me, he said proudly, 'You won't find better pig's blood anywhere on the face of the earth.'

A large bowl was placed in front of me. I dipped my hands and arms up to my elbows in the thick, dark, bubbly, steamy concoction.

We chatted amiably till dinner time and then ate heartily. Afterwards, a slave escorted me up to my bedroom. I lay down on the bed and blew out the candle. I was just dozing off when I heard a gentle tapping at the door.

'Who is it?' I called out, instantly sitting up.

'It's me, Sthenoboea.'

'What do you want, your majesty?'

'Can I come in?'

I got out of bed and unlatched the door. The queen was dressed in a sexy silk dressing gown. She was naked underneath.

'Would you like to make love to me?' she asked without ceremony, putting her lips to my ear.

'Certainly not,' I said, pushing her away. 'What do you take me for? A blaggard?'

'What's a blaggard?' she asked, placing her forefinger on her lower lip and creasing her forehead in a fetching manner.

'A blaggard? Don't you know the word? It means a worthless, contemptible person. A cad. I must ask you to leave. Your husband has been very kind to me. I'm his guest. I would never betray him.'

'Please seduce me,' Sthenoboea said, grabbing both my hands and placing them on her bosom.

I quickly tore my hands away. 'Kindly return to your room, before you get us both in trouble.'

A moment later Sthenoboea let out an ear-piercing scream.

'How could you, you blaggard!' she shouted at the top of her voice.

'Shush!' I whispered. 'Have you lost your mind?'

'How could you lay your hands on me in that indecent way? What do you take me for? A common whore?'

Before I could reply Proetus turned up with an armed guard.

'What's going on?' he demanded, darting a suspicious glance at me.

'Your guest here just tried to rape me,' Sthenoboea replied, burying her head in his breast and affecting to sob. 'He grabbed hold of me as I was passing his bedroom and dragged me inside. What a godsend that you heard my cries, my dear.'

'That's a lie!' I protested. 'I had to fight to keep your wife off me.'

'You vile miscreant,' Proetus exclaimed. 'You abominable wastrel. You foul lecher. You miserable degenerate. If you weren't a guest under my roof and protected by Zeus, I'd kill you on the spot. Instead, I'm packing you off to my friend, Iobates, the king of Lycia. He'll find an appropriate punishment for you. Wait, I'll give you a letter of introduction so he knows what he's letting himself in for.'

Proetus called for a quill and papyrus and began scribbling. Then he asked for some wax and a lighted taper, sealed the papyrus and handed it to me.

'Iobates is my father-in-law. Don't expect a warm welcome.'

'But how to I get to Lycia?'

'That's not my problem, laddie.'

For the second time in my life I was an outcast. What I didn't realise was that the letter I was carrying requested Iobates to kill me. Luckily for me, however, Iobates was equally afraid of offending Zeus by violating the laws of hospitality. He could only think of one way to avenge the alleged insult to his daughter's honour. He would set me a task that would result in my death.

'I want you to kill the Chimaera,' he said the next day.

'What's the Chimaera?'

'It's the offspring of Typhon, the youngest son of Gaia. It has the head of a lion, the body of a goat, and the tail of a dragon. It's been wreaking havoc throughout the land.'

Off I duly went. After searching for the monster for several days without laying eyes on him, I encountered an elderly seer.

'Where are you going, young man?' the seer inquired.

'I'm off to kill the Chimaera.'

'I don't envy you,' he replied. 'You'll need the services of a magical horse, if you're to have any chance of success.'

'A magical horse? Where on earth do I get hold of a magical horse at this time of night?'

'As a matter of fact there's one in the meadow over there. His name is Pegasus. He has wings. No one has ever ridden him before, so you'll need Athena's magical gold bridle to tame him. Her sanctuary is on the other side of that mountain you can see in the distance.'

I thanked the seer profusely and set out, taking long strides as is my wont. Once I'd skirted the mountain, I saw Athena's temple gleaming in the pale moonlight. Exhausted from the long walk, I flopped down, resting my head on the bottom step of the stylobate. Before falling asleep I prayed to the goddess to assist me in my quest. When I woke up next morning, lo and behold, the magical bridle was lying on the step beside me!

I jumped up, bathed in a nearby stream, and sacrificed a cow that happened to be grazing in the sanctuary to Athena, having first checked to make sure it was unblemished. I then headed back around the mountain towards the meadow with the bridle jangling at my side. Pegasus had just finished his morning exercise when I arrived and was drinking at a well. His hair was as white as the purest snow that lies on the caps of mountains.

As soon as he caught sight of me, he cantered off in fright, his hooves barely touching the ground and his wings fluttering. When he saw the bridle made of gold, however, he halted, snorted, neighed, whinnied, and tossed his head playfully. Then he trotted gaily towards me. I slipped the bridle over his neck. He knelt down on his front legs to let me mount him.

I made him gallop around the meadow a few times so that I could become used to riding him. Then, tugging his mane and patting his rump, I dug my heels into his sides, whereupon he soared majestically into the clouds at a steep angle. It was a wonderful sensation to be riding and flying at the same time, unlike anything I had ever experienced before. We flew for several hours, traversing mountain ranges, lakes, rivers, tropical rain forests, prairies, glaciers, oceans, deserts, and ice floes.

Eventually I saw the Chimaera sunning itself on a rock, flicking its tail idly back and forth. I was about to direct Pegasus to descend when the monstrous creature caught wind of us and released a vast plume of fire up into the sky. Despite the fact that we were hundreds of feet above him, it singed Pegasus' tail. His body shuddered and it was all I could do to hang onto his mane without being thrown. I steered him away and he cantered back down to earth.

For several days and nights I pondered how to overcome the Chimera's fire-breathing capability. Then suddenly I had a brainwave. I headed to the nearest blacksmith.

'Would you by any chance have a lump of iron for which you have no use?' I inquired of the swarthy fellow. 'I'll pay you handsomely for it.'

'What do you need iron for?' he asked suspiciously.

'I'm going to kill the Chimaera.'

'In that case you can have it for free. Take your pick. The odious creature devoured my parents a few days ago.'

I selected the largest lump I could carry and headed back to Pegasus, whom I'd left tethered to a tree. I grasped the reins with my free hand and we soared into the sky. This time I was careful to keep Pegasus sufficiently far above the Chimaera so that its blasts would not reach us. Then I waited for the exact moment when the monster opened its mouth to send a spurt of fire in our direction. The instant it did so I took careful aim and dropped the iron lump into its unsuspecting jaws.

The Chimaera didn't know what had hit it. On entering its throat, the iron started to melt under pressure from the fire inside the creature's belly. Very soon, molten liquid was spurting out of its jaws in all directions. The monster writhed in agony, swishing its tail back and forth in its death throes. Eventually it breathed its last, a dribble of molten saliva trickling from its maw.

When I returned to Iobates and described my heroic exploit, he was none too happy, to put it mildly. He'd been hoping the Chimaera would do away with me. He set me a number of other tasks, which he expected would lead to my death, but I accomplished them without difficulty. In the end he was forced to acknowledge that I had proven myself his benefactor.

Hubris got the better of me, however. I had come to believe that there was nothing I couldn't achieve. I became gripped by the desire to fly up to Olympus. I'd always had a hankering to see what the place looks like. I'd heard that the palaces of the gods were made of crystal with doors of solid bronze and windows encrusted with mother of pearl, not to mention the fact that the streets were reported to be paved with gold. I wanted to find out if all this was true.

Well, I never did get to find out. Long before I reached the summit, Zeus got wind of what I was up to. He dispatched a gadfly, which buzzed around Pegasus. The creature started to rear up on his hind legs, tossing his head from one side to another. Soon he was bucking like a bronco. I clung on for dear life as long as I could, but eventually even a hero's arms get tired and I lost my balance.

I plummeted towards earth through the clouds for what seemed like days. Fortunately, a canopy of trees broke my fall. Both my legs were broken in several places, however, and I've been lame ever since. I lead a pretty miserable existence these days. No one is prepared to help me for fear of offending Zeus. So, once again, I'm an exile, condemned to wander the pathless ways in a land open to the sky, traversing mile after mile through deserts and scrub lands that have never known the plough or given shelter, and painfully dragging one leg behind the other.

Steer well clear of Olympus.

Pan

I've never been welcome on Olympus either. I'm just a minor deity, you see. You have to be a member of Zeus' immediate family to qualify for a palace up there. But I'm perfectly happy living on the earth. Arcadia is my favourite haunt. It's totally bucolic.

I'm Pan. I have a human body but goat ears, goat horns and goat legs. I'm very hairy, too: exactly like a goat. I have a wispy beard as well. You might have seen me on a hillside and mistaken me for a goat. Farmers revere me. They pray to me so that their flocks and herds will multiply.

Give me a grassy hillside or a woodland grove rather than a mountaintop any day. I'm also fond of caves and grottos. I'm the son of either Zeus or Hermes. My mother was a dryad. I don't know her name and it doesn't really matter. One dryad is very much like any other. Dryads inhabit trees. They're nymphs. Nymphs come in many shapes and sizes. You also get oreads, who inhabit mountains; naiads, who dwell in lakes, rivers, and other sources of fresh water; and nereids, who live in the sea.

I also have the power to cause panic. 'Panic' comes from my name Pan. Have you ever seen a flock of sheep suddenly take flight and begin charging sheepishly in one direction? That's due to me. I can also make humans panic. I appeared to the runner Philippides on Mount Taygetus when he was on his way back from Sparta. He had sought military assistance from the Spartans and they'd refused. The Persians had landed at Marathon with a huge army and intended to reduce Athens to a pile of rubble. I told him I'd fight alongside the Athenians. I caused the Persians to panic. Without my help the Athenians wouldn't have won the battle. It turned out they didn't need the Spartans at all.

After their victory, the Athenians assigned me a cave on the north side of the Acropolis. I didn't want a temple. That's not my style. I just wanted a sacred spot where my worshippers could deposit modest offerings in my name.

I'm highly sexed. I'd be bonking all day long if I had my way. Women don't care for my hairy chest and legs, however. In order to seduce Selene, the Moon, I covered my body with a sheepskin. I didn't want her to be revolted by me. Then I drew her down to earth with a rope. It wasn't a lasting relationship, but it was fun while it lasted. Selene fell for a shepherd boy called Endymion, with whom she has had fifty daughters.

Another girl I had the hots for was a nymph called Syrinx. I promised Syrinx the moon, metaphorically speaking, but she wouldn't let me near her. She was always mocking me for my hairiness. I'm very persistent, however. One day I caught sight of her strolling on Mount Lycaon. Usually she was in the company of her fellow nymphs, but on this occasion she was alone. Highly aroused, I chased her down the mountain till we came to the River Ladon. She was screaming at the top of her voice, pleading with the river to save her. The river responded and turned her into a hollow marsh reed.

I sat down on the river bank and howled my eyes out. I hadn't intended to harm her. I'd just wanted to cuddle her. When I eventually stopped sobbing, I became transfixed by the plaintive sound made by the reeds as the wind blew through them. I grabbed a bunch of them, sliced them down the centre and joined them together, the tallest on the left, the shortest on the right. Then I blew on them. They reminded me of my darling's melancholy cries. I called my invention the syrinx in her honour.

I have a lot in common with the god Dionysus and often join in his revels. His retinue of satyrs and maenads are my close companions. That's because I'm in touch with my irrational side, just like Dionysus.

Dionysus

I'm not just 'jolly old Bacchus', as some people call me. I'm the god of lots of different things that are closely related. I'm the god of ecstasy, madness, the irrational, death, regeneration, liberation, frenzy, mass hysteria, grapes, wine, vegetation, and fertility. I'm the sap thrusting forth in a young tree, the blood pulsating in the veins of all living creatures, and the semen exploding in the ecstasy of lovemaking. I'm also the god of drama. I preside over the City Dionysia, the chief dramatic festival in Athens. God of a hundred names they call me.

I don't particularly favour stuffy old temples. I get rather claustrophobic if you stick my image in a temple. I actually prefer the open air, mountains especially. That's where mortals can attain the closest union with me. The Greek word *entheos* means 'having the god inside you'. It's where the word 'enthusiasm' comes from.

I'm also associated with mystery religion. Mystery religion promises blessedness in the Afterlife to those who undergo initiation. I'm obviously not at liberty to divulge precisely what form initiation takes. Otherwise it wouldn't be a mystery. I don't go anywhere without my *thyrsus*, a fennel stalk tipped with a pine cone, wreathed with ivy. It serves both as a weapon and as a magic wand.

I'm the diametric opposite to Apollo. Apollo stands for reason, whereas I stand for the primal instinct. It's the same deal as with Artemis and Aphrodite, also opposites. Ignore either Apollo or myself at your peril. You need both of us to lead a balanced life. Not for nothing is the wall of Apollo's sanctuary at Delphi inscribed with the words, 'Nothing in excess.'

I think I'm pretty balanced myself, despite my tendency to go off the deep end at times. Even in my gender I'm balanced. I'd describe myself as androgynous. That's why I'm popular among people who are non-binary. As you would no doubt agree, sexual identity is fluid.

Dionysus.

My first love was a boy called Ampelos. How I adored him! He happened to be riding a bull one evening – not a very sensible thing to do, I'll admit – when Selene, the Moon, sent down a gadfly to prick the bull, whereupon Ampelos lost his balance, fell off its back and was gored to death. I couldn't stop weeping when I found his mangled body. In fact I wept so much that his body sprouted into a vine. The word *ampelos* is Greek for 'vine'. My tears turned into big purple grapes.

Not only men but also women are highly susceptible to my charms. Women are confined to the home most of the time, so when they get a chance to go out they're eager to shed their inhibitions. That's where I come in. I offer complete loss of inhibition. That's why one of the names for my female worshippers is 'maenads'. The root of the word 'maenad' is *mania*, which means 'madness.' I'm good at driving people temporarily insane.

My mother was Semele, the daughter of Cadmus, the first king of Thebes. Though she was mortal, that doesn't make me any the less divine because my father is Zeus.

Zeus became attracted to her when he saw her sacrificing a bull to him on one of his altars. Instantly he knew they'd make a perfect match. He sped down to earth, introduced himself, and before long they were having an affair.

It wasn't long before Hera found out. She decided to punish my mother in the worst possible way. This she did very cunningly. She disguised herself as an old crone and took her seat on a rock by a stream of limpid water. Semele came by one day when the sun was beating down with particular ferocity.

'Dear child, could I trouble you to fill my mug with water?' Hera inquired in a croaky voice.

'Of course,' Semele replied eagerly.

She filled the mug to the brim and handed it back to her. The goddess thanked her and gulped the water down greedily. Then she looked up at Semele as if she was taking her in for the first time.

'Forgive me for saying this,' she said coyly, 'but if I didn't know better, I'd swear you were pregnant. That looks like a little bump, unless I'm much mistaken.'

'I *am* pregnant,' Semele replied blushing, placing her white arms instinctively over her womb to protect it against the evil eye.

'I knew it! I knew it!' Hera exclaimed, affecting delight. 'And who's the lucky man, if I may ask?'

Semele looked to her left and right to see if anyone was within earshot. 'Don't tell anyone, but it's the father of gods and men,' she whispered.

Hera feigned utter amazement. 'You mean Zeus? Are you serious, girl?'

'Yes indeed. I wouldn't have yielded up my virginity to a mere mortal for all the monkeys in the world.'

'What an honour! You're a very lucky girl. Just one thing, though. I don't want to burst your bubble, metaphorically speaking, but Zeus does have something of a reputation on account of his, well, his toxic masculinity, to coin a phrase. What I'm saying is that you're not the first young girl he's taken a fancy to and I very much doubt you'll be the last. If we had such a thing as a Serious Sex Offences Unit, he'd be locked up for life. Locked up for eternity, I mean.'

'I know that's the common gossip, but this is different,' Semele replied. 'Zeus loves me with all his heart. He's sworn a big oath that he'll always be faithful to me. He says I'm the most beautiful girl he's ever seen. He's promised he'll give me anything I want in the whole wide world.'

Hera could barely prevent herself from breaking into loud peals of laughter. This was classic macho, abusive behaviour on the part of her two-timing husband. She just managed to keep herself under control.

'That is very wonderful. I'm very happy for both of you and I wish you all the happiness in the world. But I still urge caution. There's only one way to find out the truth. You must ask him to make love to you just as he would if he were making love to his wife, Hera, in all his naked splendour. Then you'll know for certain if he's as good as his word. It's for your own good, dear. Will you promise to do that for me?'

Semele agreed and bade the old woman goodbye. The next time she and Zeus met up, she told him that she wouldn't make love again unless he took off every stitch of clothing. The god was thunderstruck, metaphorically speaking. He tried to wriggle out of it, of course.

'I don't think that's a good idea, Semele.'

'But you promised you'd give me anything I asked.'

'You're going to regret it, my darling.'

'If you don't, I'll never believe a word you say ever again.'

Semele wouldn't take no for an answer. She was stubborn that way. Zeus was stuck between a rock and a hard place. He'd sworn a solemn oath and his reputation was on the line. So the next time they made love he became a streak of lightning. The earth literally moved under her. She was overwhelmed and died in the throes of ecstasy. All that remained of her after they had made love was a small pile of ashes.

Zeus immediately dispatched Hermes to grab the embryo from the cinders, which he carefully bore up to Olympus. Deftly Zeus sliced open his thigh, inserted the embryo into a hollow space under the vastus medialis, and sewed the flesh back together with a needle and thread. There I remained until I came to term.

Hera was furious at having been outsmarted. After my birth, she ordered the Titans to dismember me bit by bit and devour my flesh raw. Fortunately, my grandmother, Rhea, managed to rescue my heart from their evil clutches before they could tear it into little pieces. She then scoured the earth gathering up my limbs and, long story short, when I'd been stuck back together, I was born a second time, no less miraculously than the first time.

That's why my worshippers tear live animals limb from limb and eat them raw. It's to commemorate my second birth. By doing this they acquire the vital force of the animal they devour, which enters into their bloodstream. So when they devour a bull, which is my favourite animal, they acquire the quality of a bull.

I was brought up by the nymphs on Mount Nysa. Mount Nysa is either in Libya or Egypt, or Arabia, or India. Wherever. It's in the east. That's why my worship contains so many features that are common to Eastern religions. For instance, I like to whip my devotees into a fury so that they become ecstatic. It's an Eastern thing. 'Ecstasy', from *ekstasis*, means literally 'standing outside yourself.' If you give into me fully, I'll take over your personality. Watch out! It's by standing outside themselves that actors are able to take on different roles. That's why I'm the god of drama.

I'm also the god of wine, like I said. When I discovered how to extract the precious juice of grapes and convert it into wine, Hera had another reason to be angry with me. She didn't want mortals to enjoy its benefits. So she afflicted me with madness. I had to wander up and down the earth barefoot for umpteen centuries until the effects of the madness wore off.

I eventually made up with Hera and now we're on good terms. There's no point nursing a grievance if you've got to spend all eternity nursing it. Our rapprochement came about after I intervened on her behalf concerning an argument she was having with her son, Hephaestus.

When Hera gave birth to Hephaestus, she took one look at him and threw him out of Olympus.

Hephaestus, however, was determined to have his revenge. After he was fully grown, he turned up on Olympus one evening when the gods were dining. He was hauling a large object wrapped in a sheet behind him. As soon as he entered, you could have cut the rarified air with a knife. The gods didn't know what to expect.

'Let bygones be bygones,' Hephaestus said amiably. 'You're my beloved mother and I'm your son and nothing can change that. As a token of my filial regard, I've fashioned a throne out of gold and ivory. You'll be the envy of all the gods. Please be seated. I think you'll find it fits you very snugly.'

Hephaestus whipped off the cloth to reveal his handiwork.

'Isn't it magnificent?' he inquired.

'I'm deeply touched,' Hera replied, with tears in her eyes.

The second she sat down, however, hidden adamantine straps instantly sprang forth, encasing her legs and arms. She emitted a cry of pain. Wriggle as she might, she couldn't get free. To put it mildly, she was in a right old pickle. Her violent son, Ares, tried to smash the straps but they were unbreakable.

The crippled god took his leave and went to visit a far-off people called the Smintians. It was I who finally secured her release. I journeyed to the Smintians, got Hephaestus drunk, and brought him back to Olympus on a mule with my satyrs and maenads partying alongside. He was so mellow by the time he arrived that he agreed to unshackle his mother. Ever since then the goddess has regarded me with favour.

Just think of all the good that comes to mankind as the result of alcohol. I first introduced wine to an Athenian farmer called Icarius, who received me hospitably in his cottage. Icarius took to the stuff in no time and immediately tried it out on some shepherds. He omitted to alert them to its dizzying effects, however, so they all thought Icarius had tried to poison them.

'Icarius wants to steal our sheep,' one whispered to another. 'If we drink any more of this stuff, it will kill us. Let's give him a taste of his own medicine.'

Whereupon they set upon Icarius, pinned him down, kicked him in the groin, punched him in the face, and smashed his head on the bare ground till the blood ran and he died. Then they buried him in a shallow grave under a tree.

It so happened later the same day that Icarius' daughter, Erigone, was out walking her dog. When it got near the tree, the dog pricked up its ears, sniffed, and began digging energetically. Before long it had uncovered Icarius' head. Erigone was so distressed when she realised it belonged to her father that she hurried home and immediately hanged herself.

I was so furious with the Athenians for having killed my sponsor that I inflicted them with a plague. The plague only abated when they agreed to set up a cult in honour of Icarius and Erigone.

Because I'm not a first-generation Olympian, I had a hard time gaining recognition for my divinity. One of the places most resistant to me was Thebes. In order to win the city over, I visited it with a troupe of Bacchants, aka maenads. I pretended to be a priest of Dionysus.

Cadmus' son, Pentheus, was king of Thebes. He was an arrogant sod if ever there was one. When he learned that I was recruiting local women and leading them onto Mount Cithaeron, just outside the city, he banned my cult and claimed it was cloak for nefarious practices. He even threw me into prison: the ultimate indignity.

'It's disgusting the way people like you use religion to exploit women – innocent, gullible women – for your own sordid purposes,' Pentheus snarled. 'You look more like a woman than a man. Are you one of those losers who can't make up their mind which side of the fence they're on?'

Well, that didn't do Pentheus any good, I can tell you. Soon afterwards I calmly snapped my chains and walked out of the prison free. He should have realised then and there that he was no match for me. But he didn't. He still thought he could order me around. So I decided to have some fun with him. He was easy meat. I sensed that his feigned disgust with my Bacchants was merely a cover for his prurience.

'I was wondering whether perhaps you might be curious to see what the women get up to on the mountain,' I said idly.

'Well, I am a bit curious, as a matter of fact,' he replied, trying to mask his enthusiasm. 'Could you arrange it for me?'

'I'd be delighted,' I replied, beaming broadly.

I began toying with him, just as a cat does with a mouse.

'I think you should put on a woman's dress. That way you'll be able to get really close to them.'

'Excellent idea.'

Pentheus went off and appeared back moments later. He was dressed in a pink *chiton*.

'Is my slip showing?' he inquired coquettishly.

I led him up onto Mount Cithaeron just as the sun was at its height. When we arrived, I suggested he should climb to the top of a tree so that he could have a bird's eye view of the proceedings. He didn't object. At first the scene was very peaceful. The Bacchants were at one with nature, playing with lambs, sporting with goats, striking rocks from which milk gushed forth, and so on. It was as if flora and fauna and humans all belonged to one big, happy family.

I didn't allow this idyllic scene to last long, however. Soon I started messing with the women's heads and distorting their vision, something that's easy-peasy for me to do. I made them believe that Pentheus was a lion cub. They started shaking the tree he was in and before long they had dislodged him. When he crashed to the ground, they pounced on him and began tearing him limb from limb. His screams resounded off the mountain into the valley below. The Bacchants were in a true Bacchic frenzy. The most violent of them were Pentheus' mother, Agave, and his aunts, Autonoë and Ino.

Agave returned to the palace cradling her son's head in her arms. She was proud of having killed what she thought was a lion cub with her own bare hands. It was her father, Cadmus, who gently brought her back to reality. When she came to her senses, she howled her eyes out. You can imagine my satisfaction.

I'm sorry about Ino and Autonoë. They were collateral damage. I had no sympathy for Cadmus, however. He once said it was useful for the family to promulgate the belief in my divinity and for that reason alone he'd acknowledge me. I transformed him and his wife, Harmonia, into serpents.

Cadmus, who was the brother of Europa, was the founder of Thebes.

'Have you seen your sister lately? his father Agenor asked him one morning over breakfast a week or so after she had been abducted by Zeus.

'Nope,' the lad replied without looking up from his cereal.

'Go and look for her. Don't come back unless you find her.'

'Do I have to?'

'Yes. Don't be insolent.'

Cadmus fitted out a boat and went looking everywhere for his sister without success. Eventually he decided to consult the Delphic Oracle.

'Forget your sister,' Apollo told him, 'Follow the first cow you see when you leave my sanctuary and found a city on the spot where the cow lies down.'

Cadmus left the sanctuary and found a cow. He followed it as it ambled along for half an hour before it flopped down in a meadow. He was about to sacrifice it to Athena, when the goddess appeared to him.

'Apollo told me to found a city at this spot, but how can I possibly do that on my own?' he asked her.

'Try sowing a dragon's teeth in the ground,' Athena replied, handing him a pair of golden pincers. 'That generally works.'

'OK, so all I need now is to find a dragon.'

It so happened that minutes after the encounter with Athena Cadmus came to a spring which a dragon was guarding. He picked up a rock, tiptoed up behind the dragon, and brought it down on its head. Smash! A pool of greenish blood spread around. When he had extracted the teeth with the pincers, he buried them in the soil. Immediately an army of armed men emerged. Cadmus threw a stone into their midst and they started mindlessly killing one another. Eventually there were only five of them left.

'OK, you lot,' Cadmus said. 'Now that you've had your fun, you're going to do something useful for a change. You're going to build an acropolis for me. You see the petrified bodies of your comrades over there? You can use them.'

Anyway, back to serious stuff. I had similar problems in gaining recognition in Thrace as in Thebes. The local king, Lycurgus, imprisoned my Bacchants when they were passing through his kingdom. I caused a drought and drove him mad. So he chopped up his own son, believing he was a leaf of ivy. Later, the Thracians received an oracle saying that the drought wouldn't end until Lycurgus was dead, so they cut *him* up into little pieces. Or maybe they tied his body to four horses and drove them in different directions. I forget what it was they did. Either way, I didn't have any problems with them after that. The Thracians are now among my most devoted followers. They drink unmixed wine, which Greeks normally avoid because they believe that it produces madness.

Dionysus

Inflicting madness on bad people is one of my favourite punishments. Once, when I was travelling around the world disguised as a mortal, I asked some pirates to convey me to Naxos. As soon as they got me on board, they tied me up. They were intending to sell me as a slave. They didn't know what they had bargained for. I turned the mast and the oars

Satyr showing off.

into snakes wreathed with ivy. The pirates were so terrified that they leapt into the sea, whereupon I instantly transformed them into dolphins. That's how dolphins came into existence.

I'm also very popular with satyrs. Satyrs are hairy creatures with snub noses and horses' tails. They're boisterous and flirtatious. It was an elderly satyr called Silenus who nurtured me on Mount Nysa. He's the most drunken of the lot, but he's a great teacher. Perhaps drunkenness and wisdom aren't poles apart.

While carousing in Phrygia one day as per usual, Silenus was captured by Midas, the local king. Midas had heard of Silenus' reputation for wisdom and wanted to judge for himself.

'What's the best fate for a human being?' Midas inquired when the drunken sot was brought before him.

'That's easy,' Silenus replied, burping in Midas' face. 'Not to be born. Could I have a cup of wine?'

'Only when you've told me what's the second-best fate.'

'To die as soon as possible after birth,' Silenus replied, burping again.

'Insolent fellow!' Midas exclaimed. 'Is that what your wisdom amounts to? I've half a mind to chop off your penis.'

'I wouldn't do that, if I were you,' Silenus said calmly. 'I'm a follower of Dionysus. He might take it personally. Now, how about that wine?'

Wisely, Midas released the satyr. As a mark of my gratitude, I told him he could have anything he wanted.

'Please make whatever I touch turn into gold,' Midas stupidly replied.

It doesn't take a genius to work out what the consequence of *that* wish was going to be. His food turned into gold, as did his daughter. Within seconds he was pleading with me to take away his gift. I told him to wash in the River Pactolus, which runs through Phrygia. He did so, and his power passed into the river. That's why that river is so rich in gold.

Midas carried on along his path of self-destruction, however. He became devoted to Pan, so much so that he declared openly that he preferred the sound of Pan's humble syrinx to the majestic lyre of Apollo. When Apollo found out, he scornfully observed that Midas had ass's ears, whereupon Midas' ears did indeed become those of an ass. To disguise his stupidity, the king started wearing a purple turban.

One day, when Midas was having his hair cut, however, his barber said casually, 'That's an impressive pair of ears you've got there, sire.'

Midas sat up in his chair. 'Don't you dare mention my ears to anyone, insolent fellow!' he shouted. 'If you do, I'll have your guts for garters.'

Being a barber, however, the man was unable to keep a secret of this magnitude to himself. One day he took himself to a place where no utterance could be heard and where no wheel creaked. Only the wind faintly whistled through the grass. There he dug a deep hole. Placing his mouth over it, he whispered his secret into the hole and hastily covered it over.

This worked in the short term but over time a bed of reeds grew over the hole and whenever the reeds blew in the wind, they murmured to passersby, 'Midas the king has ass's ears.'

The tragic poet Euripides wrote a play about me. I've also appeared in comedy as well. Thanks to the comic poet Aristophanes, who used me in a play called *Frogs*, the gods now call me Shittypants. That's because he depicted me as a wuss who shits when he sees all the monstrous terrors of the Underworld.

Human stupidity knows no limits. But then that's true of divine stupidity as well. Think of the mess that Zeus has made of his life, gallivanting around with all sorts of unsuitable females. As for me, I've had a few affairs in my time but I've only ever truly loved one woman, the incomparable Ariadne.

Ariadne

I'm the daughter of Minos, king of Crete. It was my father who inscribed the first lawcode. However, as you will gather from what I'm about to tell you, he wasn't responsible for the very severe anti-miscegenation law that was passed on the island later.

In centuries to come people will marvel at the splendour of our civilisation. Crete under my father headed a thalassocracy which dominated the Aegean. With any luck they'll call it 'Minoan' in honour of my father. There had never been anything approaching what you might call a civilisation in this part of the world before. I wish that were the whole of it and I could just recount the glories of our world, but my father made one big mistake and it cost him dear. That's all it takes in this life; one silly mistake. He aroused the anger of Poseidon.

My father promised to sacrifice a bull to Poseidon in return for his help in making Crete the supreme naval power. He selected the best, but just as it was being led to the altar, he experienced a change of heart. So he spared it and told his priest to fetch the second-best perfect specimen.

Poseidon was furious at being disrespected in such a public manner and he resolved to turn my parents into a laughing stock.

'If your husband wishes to fetishise that bull, I think you should too,' Poseidon announced to his wife Pasiphaë one morning when she was taking a stroll beside a bank of anemones.

She had no idea what he meant. Next morning, however, when she went out with her husband to inspect the animals on their estate, she was gripped with an insane and uncontrollable passion for the bull that Minos had spared. She started hanging around its stall, staring doe-eyed at the creature. She neglected all her familial and state duties and would no longer allow my father to touch her. Very soon her infatuation was being talked about all over the island.

In one fell swoop Poseidon had ruined my parents' life, but he'd ruined my life as well, and I'd ask you to spare a thought for me. Can you imagine the shame my family now faced? Our humiliation was unbearable. None of us dared show our faces in public.

Humiliation wasn't all that my family had to put up with, however. My father was now confronted with a highly delicate problem. Not surprisingly, my mother proved incapable of satisfying her sexual desire with the bull. She tried various positions and none of them worked. It was also painfully obvious that the bull wasn't in the least bit interested in reciprocating my mother's feelings, let alone in mating with her. Emotionally speaking, he didn't give a toss for her.

This of course made things only worse. Eventually my mother went off her food and started wasting away. What to do? My dad racked his brains to find a way around her suffering. He knew he was responsible for her affliction and he still loved her very much, which made his predicament all the more painful.

Salvation came in the person of an old Athenian friend of his called Daedalus, who turned up one day at the palace. Daedalus was the world's best sculptor, architect and craftsman. He was so skilled that his statues actually moved and had a life of their own.

My father explained my mother's predicament and asked Daedalus if he could help her out.

'Let me be sure I've got this right, Minos old chap,' Daedalus replied in his blunt Athenian way. 'You're asking me to find a way to enable your wife to mate with a bull?'

'Exactly,' my father replied, averting his gaze and blushing deeply.

'And then what?'

'What do you mean?'

'I mean what happens if I *do* find a way to achieve this end and your wife becomes pregnant?'

'Let's cross that bridge when we come to it.'

Eventually Daedalus agreed to do what my father asked and got out his drawing board. After a few days he came up with the idea of building a wooden structure in the shape of a cow; big enough for my mother to hide inside. He made it so lifelike that the bull was completely deceived. As soon as the creature saw the model, he began humping it energetically. My mother, not to put too fine a point upon it, was in raptures.

Well, one thing led to another and eventually Pasiphaë *did* become pregnant. My father urged her to abort the child, but she refused. Her belly grew to an enormous size. Eventually she gave birth to a creature which we called the Minotaur. It was half-bull and half-human. In my view the Minotaur – we never gave it a first name – should have been strangled at birth. My mother doted upon it, however, and, as always, my father gave in to her.

So now he was faced with yet another problem, just as Daedalus had warned, namely what to do with the so-called fruit of my mother's womb. He obviously couldn't leave it free to wander around the island

The Minotaur.

at will – there was no knowing what damage it might do to life and property – so he prevailed upon Daedalus to fashion a prison in which to hold the accursed creature in perpetuity.

Once again Daedalus got out his drawing board. After a month or so he came up with a brilliant solution. He would construct a vast, subterranean, maze-like structure, so complex that no living creature could ever escape from it. He called it a labyrinth because the walls were decorated with images of a double-headed axe known as a *labrys.* It took him several years to complete.

I feel very bad for Daedalus. He had no idea what he was letting himself in for when he came to visit my father. His young son, Icarus, was in attendance, and inevitably the boy became homesick. He had nothing to do all day and began pestering his father to return to Athens. But even after Daedalus had built the labyrinth, my father refused to let him go. He had become too valuable an asset.

Daedalus, however, being the supreme craftsman that he was, had a trick up his sleeve. He fashioned two pairs of wings, one for himself and one for Icarus, so that they could escape and fly back to Athens. He attached the wings to the shoulders by means of beeswax. It wasn't an ideal solution, but how else could you attach wings without driving nails into the shoulder blades? Daedalus gave Icarus strict instructions not to fly too near the sun, warning him that if he did the wax would melt.

Early one morning Daedalus and Icarus donned the wings and leapt off from a cliff. As soon as they began flapping their wings they became airborne and soared aloft into the sky. Icarus, however, forgot all about his father's warning. He started performing aerobatics, twisting and turning, doing loops and other manoeuvres. His father called out, warning him not to fly any higher, but his voice was barely audible in the thin upper air. Icarus kept flying nearer and nearer to the sun, until the inevitable happened. The wax melted and his wings detached from his body. He began plummeting earthwards and crashed headlong into the sea. Daedalus circled around the spot where Icarus had entered the water for about an hour hoping he might resurface but without success. Broken-hearted, he flew on to Athens alone.

Icarus should have learned from what happened to Phaethon. Phaethon was the son of Helios, the sun. His friends claimed that his father was just an ordinary mortal. Eventually he got fed up with being bullied so he asked his father if he could borrow his chariot to prove them wrong. Reluctantly, Helios agreed. To begin with, all went swimmingly. Before long, however, Helios' horses realised that their charioteer was completely inexperienced and incapable of controlling them so they began to bolt. Instead of keeping to their accustomed course high above

Phaethon falling from the chariot of Helios.

the earth, they descended so low that they began scorching it and setting it ablaze. This is why the peoples of Africa are dark-skinned. Fearful that the entire earth was about to burst into flames, Zeus struck Phaethon with a thunderbolt. Like Icarus, he fell into the sea and drowned.

Anyway, back to me. As if my family didn't have enough problems already, the Minotaur turned out to have a penchant for human flesh. Where could we obtain human flesh? My father could hardly sacrifice his own people. That would have caused a riot.

He solved the problem by requiring the Athenians, who were his subjects at the time, to pay tribute in the form of seven youths and seven young girls, whom they had to send to him once every seven years. The one saving grace in all this was that the Minotaur only ate meat occasionally and on special occasions.

For fourteen years the Athenians had no choice but to submit to this terrible arrangement. Eventually, however, Theseus, who was in line for the throne, decided he would put an end to it. When he arrived on Crete, the first thing Theseus did was to boast that he was the son of Poseidon. My father didn't believe him for one minute. To test the truth of his claim, therefore, he took him out in a boat, removed a gold ring from his finger, and tossed it into the sea.

'OK, dive in and retrieve my ring. I'm sure your father will protect you,' he said sarcastically.

Without a moment's hesitation, Theseus plunged into the water, scarcely making a ripple. He was gone for some time and everyone thought he had drowned. My father was about to give orders to the helmsman to head for the shore when Theseus clambered back on board, clutching the ring.

'What took you so long?' my father asked in an attempt to save face.

'I was visiting my stepmother, Amphitrite. She lives in the depths of the ocean. It takes a while to get there. So now you know I'm the son of Poseidon.'

Why there was doubt about Theseus' parenthood was because his mother, Aethra, was married to a mortal called Aegeus. Poseidon had raped Aethra when Aegeus was out of town. Aethra had been too ashamed to reveal to her husband what had happened. As a result Aegeus had always believed that Theseus was his biological son and that had been the general report.

I fell for Theseus as soon as I set eyes on him. He was tall, dark and handsome: your typical storybook prince. When he told me that he planned to kill the Minotaur and save his people, I eagerly vowed to help him.

'I hate the Minotaur,' I said. 'He's a bloody disgrace to our family.'

I explained the lie of the land of the labyrinth and handed Theseus a ball of string so that he would be able to find his way out afterwards. I suggested he should tie one end of the wool to a nail at the entrance to the maze. He wouldn't have had an exit plan if it hadn't been for me. I also gave him a sword with a blade sharp enough to pierce the Minotaur's skin, which was as tough as old nails. An ordinary sword wouldn't have penetrated it. I thought of everything, you see.

'Will you marry me?' Theseus asked, gazing soulfully into my eyes when I handed him the string and the sword.

'I will, kind sir,' I replied, without a moment's hesitation.

I was completely taken in.

As soon as Theseus emerged from the labyrinth with the head of the Minotaur, we ran down to the shore, boarded his ship, and sailed away into the proverbial sunset. I'd never been happier in my entire life. Henceforth, I thought, I won't have to live in the shadow of the family curse.

When we docked at an island called Naxos, Theseus said he needed to get fresh supplies. I wanted to stay on board, but he told me we might be there a while and urged me to explore the locality as it was very beautiful. Never suspecting he could possibly deceive me, I agreed.

I began climbing up a hill to get a good view of the island. When I reached the summit, I couldn't believe my eyes. Theseus' ship was under full sail, already half a league from the shore.

I burst into tears. He'd played me like a fool. To make matters worse, he'd made me deceive my parents. I could never return to Crete. Where could I go?

I was just about to throw myself off the cliff, when I heard the sound of drums, cymbals, pipes and other musical instruments reverberating through the air. I turned around to see Dionysus powering up the hillside in a chariot drawn by four sleek panthers. He was accompanied by a troupe of revelers: satyrs, maenads and other strange creatures.

As soon as he reached the summit, Dionysus jumped down from his chariot and said he wanted to make me his wife. I readily agreed. It was true love at first sight. Eat your heart out, Theseus!

By the way, I wasn't the only person whom Theseus mistreated bigtime. He had promised that if he succeeded in his mission and killed the Minotaur, he would hoist a white sail so that Aegeus – who still thought he was his father – would know he had survived, and that if the Minotaur had killed him, his men would hoist a black sail in mourning.

Unfathomably, Theseus hoisted a black sail. Was this a mistake or was it deliberate? Whatever the explanation, Aegeus, who was eagerly scanning the horizon, threw himself off the cliff when he made out the black sail on the horizon.

Along with Aeacus and Rhadamanthus, my father is one of the three judges down in Hades. They don't pass judgement on whether the dead should go to Heaven or Hell because we don't believe in that sort of thing, and the overwhelming mass of humans end up in the same dreary place. Instead the judges arbitrate among the dead whenever they have disputes. The dead are extremely litigious. They haven't got anything better to do except quarrel among themselves. The judges are subject to Hades and Persephone, king and queen of the Underworld.

Persephone

I'm the wife of Hades, also known as Pluto, lord of the dead. The name 'Hades' applies both to my husband and to his realm, the dark house of the dead. There isn't much to do down here. Hades and I don't have any children because Hades – here I mean the land of the dead – doesn't support life. Quite aside from that existential problem, my husband is so much older than I am, and, frankly, he can hardly get it up. Most of the time I'm bored out of my mind. The only good thing is that I don't have to spend *all* eternity in Hades, but only a portion thereof, for reasons I'll explain in a moment.

The dead are pretty boring as well. I try to have as little to do with them as possible. They have shrill voices like bats and their limbs are very feeble. When they try to touch anything or anyone, their hands go right through the object or person as if it wasn't there. That's particularly frustrating for them whenever they encounter someone they loved back on earth. Both parties rush forward to embrace one another and they end up zooming through each other with their arms outstretched. They usually try three times, before they give up in despair.

To make matters worse, the dead are all so bloody negative. I admit that's not entirely their fault because they're caught in a time warp. The future doesn't exist for them. The consequence is that they're always moping about how they *might* have lived their lives. 'If only' are a corpse's favourite words. You want to say to them, 'Get over it and move on,' but there's nothing for them to move on to. That's the worst part of being dead. It's no surprise that I don't think I've ever seen a happy corpse. They miss their families and friends, and if anyone comes visiting from the world above or if a recent decedent arrives, they flock around, pumping the person for all the latest gossip. It's the only time they get news about what's going on in the world above.

70

The one consolation – if indeed it's a consolation – is that the dead are all in the same boat, metaphorically speaking. What I mean is that they don't get rewarded or punished in Hades according to how they lived on earth. Good and bad suffer an identical fate. The only exceptions are those really big sinners like Tantalus, Ixion, Tityus and Sisyphus. Oh, and the forty-nine Danaids. You'll hear about them in due course. Plus there are a few valiant warriors who end up either in Elysium or the Isles of the Blessed.

Another sad thing is that the dead know that Hades is the best place for them, even though it's so unpleasant. If someone dies and is left unburied, she or he will be denied access to the Underworld. They'll have to wander up and down the banks of the River Styx for thousands of years. That's why Oedipus' daughter, Antigone, was so upset when her uncle, Creon, declared that the corpse of her brother, Polyneices, couldn't be buried. That's also why the ghost of Patroclus appeared to Achilles in his sleep and begged him to bury him. And that, too, is why relatives of the dead place an obol between the teeth of the corpse before the funeral. An obol is pretty worthless, but you need to give one to Charon so that he'll ferry you across the River Styx into Hades in his crappy old boat. If the old boy doesn't get his obol, he'll leave you to rot: literally. He's very particular that way.

Enough about the dead. Let's talk about me. I'm the daughter of Zeus and Demeter. They're actually brother and sister, though incest is not unusual among Olympians. My mother is the goddess of the harvest. She's a very important goddess. Bread-eaters couldn't survive without her intervention. Farmers sacrifice to my mother in the hope that she'll give them a good harvest. She taught mortals how to sow and till the ground. They would never have discovered agriculture if it hadn't been for her. Previously all bread-eaters were nomadic.

Mine is a story for the ages. It's happened millions of times over. That's why it's so important. I'd just turned thirteen. I was innocently plucking narcissi in a meadow one afternoon in midsummer when a rushing wind swirled around me on all sides. I looked up at the sky and saw a four-horse chariot careening down to earth at full speed. It was moving so fast that I didn't have a chance to get out of its way. Just as the chariot landed, the driver extended his giant right arm and gathered me up in his hairy embrace. We sped on for a mile or so and then the chariot entered a dark cave and plummeted down a subterranean tunnel. We seemed to be hurtling towards the centre of the earth at breakneck speed. Suddenly we came to a screeching halt. The air smelt damp and there was a strong wind blowing.

'Welcome to Hades,' my abductor said, stepping down from the chariot and offering me his hand.

He had a courtly air about him and pleasant manners, but he was about one hundred times my age. Certainly old enough to be my great-great-great-endlessly-great-grandfather. He had copper-coloured hair, a very long beard, and unhealthily, pallid skin.

'I don't know what your little game is, but I demand that you return me to earth this instant,' I said in a peremptory tone, doing my best to keep my composure.

'Don't you recognise me, Persephone? I'm your uncle, Pluto. I'm lord of the dead. This is my realm and I have chosen you to be my queen. Well, what do you say? "Thank you" might be appropriate.'

'Thank you, but I have no intention of being either your queen or anyone else's queen for that matter. I want to go home; right now. My mother will be worried sick. She's extremely powerful and she has a perfectly dreadful temper. I should know. Besides I don't much like it down in your so-called realm. It smells to high heaven.'

At that I stamped my foot, thereby creating a putrid-smelling cloud of dust that gave me a coughing fit.

'Yes, the dead are a bit malodorous,' Pluto conceded. 'There's nothing I can do about that. That's the condition in which they arrive here. You'll get used to the smell eventually. And to the dust.'

'Eventually? Didn't you hear me? I demand that you take me back up to earth right now.'

Pluto patted me affectionately on the shoulder. I squirmed at his touch.

'You're just going to have to make the best of things, my dear,' he said affably.

Meanwhile, back on Olympus, as I later discovered, my mother was in a right old tizzy, to put it mildly. She started looking for me everywhere. None of the gods had any idea where I'd gone. Eventually she arrived at Eleusis, just to the west of Athens. She had disguised herself as an old woman. She knocked on the door of the palace of Keleus and Metaneira, the king and queen of Eleusis.

The queen had recently given birth to a baby boy called Demophoön and my mother offered to nurse him. Metaneira agreed.

The boy grew lustily, due to the fact that my mother nourished him on ambrosia, which as you probably know is what the gods live on. After Metaneira had gone to bed each night, she would place Demophoön close to the fire so that his mortal flesh would burn away.

One night, however, Metaneira got up out of bed to let the cat out only to discover – as she thought – my mother roasting her son in the fire.

'What in the gods' name are you're doing, you witch?' she screamed, wresting Demophoön from her. 'You're a perfect monster. You're depraved! To think that I trusted you!'

'You silly woman,' Demeter replied, shedding her disguise and revealing herself in all her glory. 'I was in the process of making your son immortal. But now you've ruined my spell.'

'Forgive me,' Metaneira said, instantly abasing herself.

'You must establish a festival at Eleusis in my honour,' Demeter said.

So that's how the Eleusinian Mysteries came to be established. If a mortal becomes initiated in these mysteries, it's guaranteed that she or he will enjoy a better life in Hades. Thousands become initiated every year.

My mother continued wandering over the earth without success. The days lengthened into months and the months into a full year. She neglected her duties as goddess of the harvest, with the result that nothing grew on earth. She retired to Mount Olympus and locked herself in her bedroom, keeping the shutters closed day and night. The sky remained perpetually cloudy and the sun was rarely seen.

Before long, all living creatures were facing starvation. The gods also began feeling the pinch. Mortals were no longer burning thigh pieces wrapped in fat on their altars. They hadn't had a sniff in months. They were scarcely better off than the humans.

My mother might have neglected her duties forever, were it not for the fact that Helios came to her one day and revealed what had happened. Helios sees everything in his course across the sky each day and he'd witnessed my abduction. He further revealed that Zeus had secretly connived in it.

As soon as my mother learned what had happened, she was filled with rage. She demanded to see Zeus instantly.

'If you don't get Hades to release Persephone from his evil clutches immediately, crop production will cease for all time. Everything is already dying down on earth, as you know. But it'll only get worse. Not only will there be no sacrifices, but you can also kiss goodbye to temples and statues and votive offerings and festivals and libations and prayers. In short, immortal life as you know it will cease.'

My mother can be quite scary when she wants to be and she certainly put the frighteners on Zeus. He didn't want to forego the rich sacrifice of 100 oxen that was made to him at Olympia every year among other rich pickings, so he summoned Hades from Hades and read him the riot act.

'This won't do, old chap,' Zeus said, shaking his head gravely and causing thunderbolts to fly in all directions. 'You're going to have to let Persephone go. Demeter is on my case, and if I let you get away with this, there'll be all hell to pay.'

Pluto bowed his head and promised to do as he was bid. When he returned to Hades, he told me I was free to leave. He pretended to be remorseful. He even apologised for abducting me.

'I'm glad you've finally seen reason,' I said. 'About time too.'

'Before you go, my dear, you'll need to eat something. It's a long way back up to earth and you'll be bound to feel queasy as you speed to the upper air. It's going to be a bumpy ride. Here, eat this pomegranate.'

'I don't like pomegranates,' I replied. 'They don't agree with me.'

'Just eat the seeds then. At least they'll prevent motion sickness.'

I did as I was bid. Then I climbed into his chariot. Pluto flicked his whip and his horses hurtled back up to earth. I was so thrilled to see the sunlight again when we emerged from his subterranean domain that I even gave him a peck on the cheek as I got down onto the solid earth.

As soon as my mum saw the chariot arrive, she ran towards me. This caused the sun to break through the clouds. Trees instantly grew leaves, wheat and barley shot up from the ground, fruit ripened, flowers sprung, and birds began chirping. We hugged and kissed.

'You must be hungry after your long journey,' she said.

'I'm not, as a matter of fact. I ate some pomegranate seeds and they were curiously filling,' I informed her.

Mum stopped in her tracks. 'You did what?' she said. 'Don't you know that if you eat *anything* in Hades, even a few seeds, you are bound to the kingdom of the dead forever.'

'How could I possibly know that? You never told me.'

74

'I thought everyone knew that, you stupid girl!'

So that in a nutshell was that. There wasn't a thing anyone could do about it.

Mum had to come to a compromise with Hades. For five months every year she mourns my absence, since I'm confined to the Underworld and have to play the role of a dutiful wife. For the other seven months I live on Mount Olympus, which makes her very happy. That's why the flowers blossom and the crops grow. And so it will be for all time. And that is the reason why we have a division of the year into summer and winter.

After she had caused the earth to come back to life, mum entrusted mysteries to the people of Eleusis. They are known only to those who have been initiated, so I can't say anything about them. All I can say is that they will enjoy special privileges in Hades.

'Happy are those who have seen these things,' begins the hymn which was composed in celebration of these rites, though what these things are will forever remain secret.

Just occasionally a live human descends to Hades. One such was Orpheus. Orpheus had the sweetest voice in the world. He could produce a diminuendo to die for: literally. He could also hit the high Cs. He was able to charm animate and inanimate objects alike – bears, lions, insects, birds, woods, rivers – even stones.

Orpheus married Apollo's daughter, the nymph Eurydice. He loved her passionately. If ever there was true love, this was it. Shortly after their wedding, Eurydice was sitting in a lush sward making a daisy chain when a drunken satyr caught sight of her and tried to rape her.

'You're a cutie,' the satyr said in a feeble attempt at flattery.

He had no idea she was married and wouldn't have cared less if he had. Eurydice managed to escape his clutches by scratching his cheeks with her sharp nails, only to trip and fall into a nest of vipers. One of the vipers bit her in the ankle. Before long her face became numb and she had difficulty breathing. Within an hour she was dead.

Orpheus was inconsolable. He couldn't live without his Eurydice so he descended to Hades in the hope that he might be able to bring her back to earth. He had no trouble circumventing Cerberus, the fifty-headed dog that guards the entrance to Hades, charming it with his mellifluous voice so that it rolled over onto its back with its paws in the air, its tongue lolling out of its mouth.

Once he arrived in the Underworld, Orpheus cleared his throat and began singing a love song. I'll never forget it. It was the most beautiful sound I have ever heard. My husband, who is usually emotionally dead, was so moved that even he began sobbing. All the denizens of the Underworld began weeping as well. Before long there wasn't a dry eye in the realm.

The upshot was that my husband agreed to release Eurydice on the strict condition that Orpheus didn't look back at her until they had emerged into the bright light of day.

The loving couple began their ascent to the upper air, Eurydice several feet behind. Just as he saw the light at the end of the tunnel, however, Orpheus couldn't refrain from turning around to make sure she was following.

'Nearly there, my love,' he said, squeezing her hand and glancing into her eyes.

In that instant his beloved slipped away and was spirited back to Hades, a faint cry escaping from her lips. Orpheus tried to descend a second time, but Cerberus was on the alert and snarled threateningly when he approached.

Orpheus became a complete recluse. He withdrew to the mountains of Thrace. Although many beautiful women sought out his company, he would have nothing to do with them. He found some pleasure in the company of young men and that is why so many Thracians are homosexuals. However, his greatest consolation was in music, which he continued to compose in honour of Eurydice. Wherever he went, rivers and rocks followed him around, haunted by the heavenly melodies he produced.

His musical gift landed him in big trouble, however. One day a group of Bacchants, devotees of Dionysus, heard Orpheus singing and crept towards him. At first, they were charmed by the pure lyricism of his music and were reduced to floods of tears. Moments later, however, he whipped them up into a fury by singing a song of expressive chromatism that lacked a common tonic. It was so thrilling, so emotionally intense and so overpoweringly poignant that they were unable to control themselves. In a frenzy they tore him limb from limb, indifferent to his anguished cries.

The Bacchants scattered his limbs far and wide. They tossed his head into the River Hebrus, where it floated out to sea, still singing plaintive songs in honour of Eurydice. The head finally washed up on the island of Lesbos.

A serpent, which took exception to the singing, was about to bite it, but Apollo was on the lookout and turned the serpent to stone. The Muses gave the head an honourable burial. That is why so many great poets have been born on Lesbos, including the poetess Sappho, one of the very greatest of them all.

There's a happy ending of sorts to this tale, however. Being truly dead, Orpheus could now descend to Hades and be reunited for all eternity with his beloved, even though the pair could not embrace. To celebrate his musical genius, Zeus set his lyre in the sky as the constellation Lyra.

Visitors to Hades always liven things up, but they're few and far between. Theseus was here a while back. So was Odysseus. So was Heracles, on a mission to abduct Cerberus.

Heracles

I'm certainly not one to boast but if you were to describe me as the greatest of the Greek heroes, you wouldn't be far wrong. I'm a symbol of the indomitability of the human spirit. I've not had it easy. Far from it. You try cleaning the Augean stables, for starters. And that was just *one* of my twelve labours.

Zeus decided he wanted to sire a son who would be all-powerful and he vowed that that son should be a descendant of Perseus. He selected Perseus' granddaughter, Alcmene, as a suitable mother. One night when Alcmene's husband, a Theban called Amphitryon, was away fighting the Taphians, Zeus entered Alcmene's bedroom disguised as her husband, while she was reading in bed by the flickering light of an oil lamp.

'I'm home, honey,' he announced, emulating Amphitryon's haughty tone of voice.

'That was quick,' Alcmene said, sitting up. 'I wasn't expecting you till tomorrow at the earliest, dear.'

'I just can't keep my hands off you,' Zeus replied. 'That's what motivated me to get back double-quick. The Taphian king had a magical lock of hair which rendered him invulnerable, but I managed to snip it off. I won't bother you with the details. The important thing is I'm here now and I can't wait to get down to business with you.'

Alcmene threw back the counterpane and Zeus hopped in beside her. Legend has it that he made the night three times as long to satisfy his lust for her. When Amphitryon returned a few days later, he, too, was eager to have intercourse with his wife. Alcmene, who was none too bright, didn't work out what was going on, even though Amphitryon proceeded to tell her a very different story about how he vanquished the Taphian king. This was how my twin brother, Iphicles, was conceived, by Amphitryon.

When Hera learned that Zeus had fathered a son who would be all-powerful, she hit the proverbial roof. It was bad enough that her husband had sired another child out of wedlock, but what made it much worse was that he would enjoy such prestige. Accordingly she dispatched Eileithyia to delay my birth and accelerate that of my cousin, a pathetic, weasel-like specimen called Eurystheus.

To make me deathless, Zeus placed me on Hera's breast while she was sleeping. I began sucking greedily. Instantly she awoke and tore my gums away from her nipple. It was too late, however. The damage was done. I'd already gobbled down pints of creamy milk; enough to last an immortal lifetime. Droplets of it kept trickling down her breasts. Hence the trail of stars that is called the Milky Way.

Hera wasn't done yet with trying to thwart Zeus, however. She sent two huge snakes to attack me when Iphicles and I were lying in our crib. Iphicles cried out as the snakes slunk towards us, their tongues flicking. I sprang to infant attention and fearlessly grasped each in my podgy hands and strangled both to death.

When the blind Theban seer Teiresias heard what I had done, he predicted that I would one day join the gods on Olympus. No pressure, eh?

I'm by far the most muscular of the heroes. Just take a gander at my rippling sinews. I believe in keeping in shape. I'm a prime example of bigorexia. I don't keep fit just for the heck of it, however. The world is a much safer place because of me. If I hadn't put my muscles to good use, mortals would still be living in terror of monsters. But it's not all sweetness and light being me. It never is if you're a hero. There's also a dark side to my character. I've tried to repress it, but it keeps rearing its head. I first went off the rails when I was an adolescent.

My surrogate father, Amphitryon, had determined to give me a good education. He therefore shipped me off to the centaur Chiron, famous, as you've probably heard, for his pedagogical skills. Chiron thought that if I learned to play the lyre, it would help to tame my wild nature. I hated the instrument with a passion. One day my music teacher, a crotchety old sod called Linus, got so frustrated with my inability to master the basics that he clipped me around the ear. I wasn't going to stand for that. I picked up a stool and brought it down with such force that it smashed his skull.

Chiron had no choice but to kick me out of his house. To atone for my crime, I performed the first of my very long list of very good deeds by killing a lion, which had been ravaging Thebes. In gratitude, Creon, the king, permitted me to marry his daughter, Megara.

All went well to begin with. We were happily married and had several children. Hera, however, decided to get her revenge on Zeus by messing with my mind. I imagined there were enemies lurking under the bed and hiding behind the tapestries. I grabbed my bow and began randomly shooting anything that moved, indifferent to the demented howls and shrieks of my victims. When the fit left me, I slumped to the ground and saw the full horror of what I had done. My wife and children lay dead at my feet.

I was mortified. I felt my life was over. I went to the Delphic Oracle to atone for my heinous crime.

'Purification isn't enough,' Apollo informed me. 'You're going to have to perform some labours for your cousin, Eurystheus, the king of Tiryns.'

'For Eurystheus?' I exclaimed in horror. 'You can't be serious. The man's a complete wuss. Please make it for someone else. This is so degrading.'

'Wuss or no wuss, he's a descendant of the House of Perseus and he was actually born before you. Zeus, as you know, decreed that the first-born will be all-powerful. Oracle-wise you have no choice.'

'How many labours must I perform?'

'Let's see. Ten is a nice round number.'

So I set off for Tiryns.

'Apollo has told me to perform some labours for you,' I said when I was ushered into Eurystheus' presence. 'You probably know who I am.'

'Indeed I do,' Eurystheus replied with an air of condescension. 'I understand you need to atone for the dreadful crimes you've committed by putting your muscles to good use. I've been drawing up a list of labours. The first is to slay the Nemean lion. That should keep you out of trouble.'

So off I went into the wilds of Nemea. After several days I managed to track down the aforesaid lion by following a warm trail of blood. I came across the beast licking its slavering chops at the mouth of a cave, surrounded by gristle and bone. I extended my bow, carefully aimed an arrow at its heart, and let go. To my dismay the arrow bounced straight back with almost equal force. The animal snarled, growled,

Heracles wrestling with the Nemean lion.

rose to its paws, fixed its eyes on me, and leapt towards me. I threw away my bow, raised my club, and struck it on the crown of its head. The club, too, rebounded. It was like hitting rubber. I dropped my club, wrestled the animal to the ground, twisted its neck, and strangled the life out of it. My mission completed, I tried to flay it with a knife. This, however, proved impossible, due to the fact that its pelt was impervious to my blade. Eventually I hit upon the solution of stripping off its pelt by using its own claws. Voilà! Whenever you see a hero wearing a lion's head you'll know it's either me or my descendant, Alexander the Great.

The next labour Eurystheus assigned me was to slay the nine-headed Hydra that was devouring the people of Lerna. This was a particularly tricky assignment owing to the fact that if you cut off one of the monster's heads, two immediately grew in its place. I got around this logistical impasse by enlisting the services of my nephew, Iolaus. As soon as I cut off one of the heads, Iolaus cauterised the wound to prevent two heads from growing back.

Labour number three was to bring back the giant Erymanthian boar to Eurystheus. I tied its legs and carried it all the way to Tiryns on my shoulders. When I dumped it at his feet, he was so petrified that he hid in a storage jar. What a pussy!

Either before or after that labour – I forget the order – I captured the Ceryneian hind, which was roaming wild through Arcadia. It took me a whole year to track it down. I eventually cornered it in the land of the Hyperboreans, a race of giants who live beyond the place where Boreas, the North Wind, has his abode. There wasn't much point to this labour, except that no one else had been able to catch the stag, so yet again I proved my prowess.

My fifth labour was to shoot the man-eating birds that haunted the marshes of Stymphalia. These obnoxious creatures had bronze beaks and bronze feathers. The worst of it, however, was that they released poisonous dung from their bottoms. Talk about being shat upon from a great height. To make matters worse, it was impossible to get within half a mile of them because of the quagmires that they inhabited. Every time I tried to approach, I got stuck in a quagmire. I couldn't have succeeded if Athena hadn't given me a rattle. When I shook the rattle, the birds took refuge on a nearby mountain as they couldn't stand the noise. I stormed up the mountain while the noise continued to reverberate and took careful aim. Ping, ping, ping! Within moments the mountain was littered with feathery corpses. Another job well done.

My next labour was to clean the stables of King Augeas in Elis. Augeas, the son of Helios, had more cattle than anyone else in Greece – bulls, cows, horses, sheep and goats – and he hadn't cleaned his stables in years. The muck was mountainous. As you will have gathered, I'm not just brawn and no brains, however. Eurystheus was hoping that the task would break my back, and it would have, if I'd just relied on my shovel. Instead I knocked a big hole in opposite walls of the stables. Then I diverted two local rivers to flush all the muck out. I'd made Augeas promise he would reward me by giving me one-tenth of his herd. He tried to renege on the deal, but I forced him to pay up. However, when Eurystheus found this out, he claimed that this labour didn't count owing to the fact that I'd received recompense. So he set me two more.

My seventh labour was to capture a mad bull that was rampaging through Crete, destroying crops and smashing walls. No problem.

Number eight was to steal some mares that Diomedes, king of Thrace, had trained to devour human flesh.

Number nine was to get hold of the magic belt that Hippolyta, the queen of the Amazons, wore. You'll be hearing more about the Amazons later. Hippolyta took quite a fancy to me and would have given it to me voluntarily, had it not been for Hera, who disguised herself as Hippolyta and pretended to be plotting against me. I therefore slew the queen, though to my credit I later regretted it.

My tenth labour was to seize the cattle that belonged to the three-headed monster Geryon. I shot an arrow through all three of Geryon's foreheads and brought the cattle back to Eurystheus, who sacrificed them to Hera.

My final two labours involved me in journeys to lands where no man had trod before. The first was to acquire the golden apples that are guarded by the Hesperides at the ends of the earth. For this I needed the help of Atlas, the Titan, who supports the earth, because the Hesperides are his daughters. Atlas, who turned out to be a crafty fellow, agreed to go to the ends of the earth and fetch the apples on condition that I supported the weight of the earth on my back while he was gone.

'I've got a suggestion,' he remarked when he returned from Hesperia clutching the apples. 'Why don't I save you the trouble of having to make the long trek to Tiryns by bringing the apples to Eurystheus myself? That way you can take the weight off your feet a bit longer, metaphorically speaking. Does that sound like a plan?'

'That's very generous of you,' I replied. 'Apart from the tediousness of the journey, I've no desire to set eyes on Eurystheus. I can't stand the fellow. He's a total loser. You'll be doing me a really big favour. Are you sure don't mind? Just one thing. Would you mind supporting the weight of the earth for a few seconds while I adjust my shoulder pad? Antarctica is cutting into my clavicle and I'm afraid it may damage my cervical vertebrae.'

Atlas foolishly agreed. As soon as he took over, I grabbed the apples out of his hand and scarpered, leaving him holding the baby, metaphorically speaking.

My final labour was to descend to Hades and abduct the three- or nine- or or fifty- or one-hundred headed dog Cerberus. This was the toughest labour of all. I put the irascible creature into my famous stranglehold and it lost consciousness. Then I tied it up in the adamantine chains I'd brought with me. I was just about to head back to the upper air when I happened to encounter the ghost of the hero Meleager.

'Would you marry my sister?' he inquired out of the blue.

'I don't know. Is she good-looking?' I asked.

'She's stunning,' he replied.

And so I agreed.

While down in Hades I also took the opportunity to rescue Theseus, who was strapped to the Chair of Forgetfulness. This was his punishment for having tried to abduct Persephone from Hades. I would have rescued his friend, Pirithoüs, strapped down in an adjoining chair, but whenever I grabbed him, the Underworld shook so violently that I had to leave him where he was for fear the upper world might fissure and crack open.

Once back in Tiryns, I tossed the canine at the feet of Eurystheus. He was so scared that he leapt up from his throne and again took refuge inside a storage jar. I picked up the jar, shook him out and forced him to release me from my servitude.

Heracles abducting Cerberus from Hades.

I've performed a lot of other tasks in the course of my lifetime. One was when King Laomedon refused to pay Apollo and Poseidon for the help they had given him in constructing the walls of Troy. They'd punished him by sending a sea monster. Laomedon said he would give up his daughter, Hesione, if only they would call off the sea monster. Instead I killed it with one blow of my club.

My least edifying labour involved a pair of dwarfs known as the Cercopes. They had snuck up on me while I was relaxing on a river bank and tried to steal my bow and arrows, but I caught hold of them and roped them on either end of a pole. I threw the pole over my shoulders and started walking, the Cercopes hanging upside down, swaying back and forth. I hadn't gone more than a few yards when they both started laughing.

'What's so funny?' I asked.

'Your bottom,' they replied, tittering.

'What's so funny about my bottom?'

'It's black.'

'So would yours be if you'd been around the world doing good deeds like I have,' I replied testily. 'It's tanned, that's all.'

This sent the dwarfs into paroxysms of laughter. In the end I got so fed up with them that I let them go.

After that I decided it was time to marry Meleager's sister. Deianeira, the girl in question, was stunningly beautiful. She had slanting almond-shaped eyes and raven black hair down to her navel. The only problem was that the river god Acheloüs had already declared his love for her. Acheloüs had the ability to take multiple shapes. This wasn't a problem for an old pro like me, however. I challenged him to a wrestling contest and won hands down.

On our way to Tiryns we encountered a river in full flood. A centaur called Nessus offered to carry Deianeira across. I thought this was a very generous offer and readily agreed. I was feeling exhausted and decided to kip. I had only just drifted off when I was awoken by the sound of Deianeira screaming.

'Get your legs off me, you filthy centaur!'

I grabbed my bow and arrow and shot Nessus through the heart. As he was expiring, he handed Deianeira a vial containing his blood. He told her that if ever she suspected that my ardour for her was waning, she should mix the blood with a tablespoonful of olive oil and it would instantly revive.

Bottom line: a girl should never trust a centaur. Still, I confess I do have a wandering eye. I just can't help myself. A few months later I returned home with a girl called Iole. We'd been an item before I married Deianeira. I'd proposed to Iole, but her father, Eurytus, had forbidden the marriage, fearing I would kill her, just as I'd killed Megara.

I could tell Deianeira was pretty annoyed but she didn't raise any objection. Then one day my herald, Lichas, happened to espy me and Iole making out in a barn.

'I think you should know that your husband is having an affair with Iole,' he told Deianeira.

'I thought as much,' she replied. 'He's been giving the marriage bed the old heave-ho of late.'

Deianeira went to her closet and took out the vial containing Nessus' blood. She smeared the blood on a tunic that I was planning to wear next day at a sacrifice to Zeus.

As soon as I began the sacrifice, the heat from the flames caused the poison to flare up. My skin began erupting in ulcers that swelled up and burst. I died in terrible agony. Just before I expired, I grabbed Lichas and hurled him off a jagged cliff into the sea. When Deianeira found out that she had caused my death, she was, of course, devastated. She tore out her hair and lacerated her breast with her nails. Then she went into our bedroom and hanged herself.

With my last gasp I told my son, Hyllus, to marry Iole. Hundreds of years later my great-great-grandsons invaded the Peloponnese. That's how I came to be the ancestor of the Dorians, the people who inhabit the Peloponnese, including the Spartans, who are immensely proud to trace their descent back to me.

As soon as I had breathed my last, I was wafted up onto Mount Olympus. Hera finally made peace with me and gave me her daughter Hebe, goddess of Youth, to marry.

It's true that I've screwed up at times, but when you add up all that I've done to improve the lot of the human race, I rank head and shoulders above anyone else, excepting only the Titan Prometheus.

Prometheus

I never did run with the pack. I sided with Zeus in his war against my brothers and sisters: the war we call the Titanomachy. When it ended, Zeus punished the other Titans severely. He condemned Atlas to having to support the heavens on his shoulders.

My alliance with Zeus didn't last long, however. As soon as he declared himself top god, he started behaving tyrannically. It broke my heart to see how he disregarded wretched mortals so I decided to do something about it.

The first thing I did was to ensure that humans didn't waste all their food on sacrifices. I sacrificed an ox and separated the meat into two piles. In one pile I put the stringy thigh bones covered in fat and in the other the juicy meaty pieces wrapped in the entrails. I made it look as if the pile with the stringy thigh bones was the tastier. I asked Zeus to choose which pile he preferred. He pointed to the bones covered in fat, just as I was hoping. This is why mortals always get the better portion of the meat that they sacrifice and why the gods always get the lousy thigh bones. It makes sense. The gods don't actually eat the meat. They merely snort down the savour of the smoke.

When Zeus found out that I had tricked him, he went ballistic. He denied mortals access to fire. They couldn't cook, couldn't make bread, couldn't manufacture anything, and could hardly keep body and soul together. Once again I came to their rescue. I stole a spark of fire from Mount Olympus, hid it inside a fennel stalk, and carried it down to earth. Humans commemorate my act of generosity by holding annual torch races in my honour.

My third gift to mortals – no less valuable – was depriving them of knowledge of the future. If mortals knew what was in store for them, they'd simply give up. Knowledge of the future is a terrible curse.

Zeus – again – was furious. He ordered Hephaestus to fashion what he called a woman. He named her Pandora. He instructed all the gods and goddesses to give Pandora a gift. Athena gave her a silvery garment, an embroidered veil, and a crown of flowers. Aphrodite gave her sexual allurement, which made her seductive to the nth degree. Hephaestus endowed her with cunning and deceitfulness, and so on. Hence her name, which means 'Having all gifts'. Zeus added curiosity to her character traits. He called her 'a beautiful evil'. It was his intention that she would wreak havoc in the world.

He presented Pandora to the most stupid person in the world, namely my brother, Epimetheus. I'd warned Epimetheus never to accept any presents from Zeus, but he wouldn't listen. He never listens. He always lives up to his name, which means 'Afterthought'. I, by contrast, always think ahead. Hence my name, which means 'Forethought'.

Epimetheus owned a large earthenware jar attractively decorated with mythological scenes, which he always kept sealed. He told Pandora that under no conditions should she open it. Thanks to Zeus, however, she was incorrigibly curious and just had to open it. As soon as she did so, all the evils that beset the human race flew out: disease, hard work, war, famine, drought, old age, and so on. Only hope, which lay at the bottom, remained inside. That is the reason why mortals who lead miserable lives hope against hope that things will get better. That counts for a lot, because if you extinguish hope, there's nothing left to life.

Because of my gifts to mortals, Zeus ordered Hephaestus to chain me to a rock in the Caucasus Mountains. Every day he sent his eagle to prey on my liver, thereby causing a deep wound, but every night my wound healed because I'm immortal.

The only thing that gave me hope was the fact that I knew the identity of a mortal woman who was destined to give birth to a son mightier than his father. Zeus was desperate to find out who this was in case the mother turned out to be someone he was planning to sleep with. He swore to release me if I would reveal her name. Despite the agony I was in, however, I refused.

Heracles secured my release in the end. He stopped off in the Caucasus Mountains on his way to Hesperia in search of the golden apples and happened to come my way. I advised him to consult Atlas,

Prometheus being devoured by an eagle.

whose daughters guarded the apples. He was so grateful for this information that he shot the eagle and cut through my bonds. Free at last!

Heracles and I have done a lot for the human race. Most people you encounter in myth undertake adventures simply to win glory. A prime example is Jason. He could have done *so* much good if he'd put his mind to it, but nothing he ever did with his prowess did any good to anyone.

Jason

Recovering the Golden Fleece was my greatest achievement, possibly the greatest achievement of all time, but that isn't the only reason why I have a big reputation among the heroes.

My father, Aeson, the king of Iolcus, had been deposed by his half-brother, Pelias. The only reason why Pelias hadn't killed me at birth was because my mother told him I was stillborn. She sent me away to be educated by the centaur Chiron.

Most people look down their noses at centaurs because they're hybrids: human head and torso and the rest horse. Most of them are pretty disorderly. When a Lapith invited centaurs to his wedding, they tried to rape all the women. Chiron wasn't like that at all, however. He was very civilised. That was because he had human front legs.

Centaurs fighting.

He was therefore more human than horse. Most centaurs have horse legs front and back. They are therefore more horse than human.

Chiron nonetheless came to a sticky end. One day Heracles was dining with a centaur called Pholus and asked his host if he could have some wine. Pholus had taken the pledge as he knew that its effects were ruinous on centaurs, but he couldn't refuse his distinguished guest, particularly since he was just about to undertake his fourth labour. So he cracked open a cask that Dionysus had given him for special occasions. The bouquet that the wine released was so strong that centaurs from miles around pricked up their ears and trotted to his house. They kicked down the front door and began raiding his cellar. Heracles killed as many of them as he could, but one of his arrows accidentally struck Chiron in the heart.

That was the end of my education. When I turned eighteen, I determined to reclaim the throne of Iolcus. On my way to Pelias' palace, I encountered a wizened old hag dressed in a threadbare cloak. She was attempting to cross a river that was in full spate. Being a gentleman, I offered to help her. I lifted her onto my back and began wading across. She weighed almost nothing. I nearly got swept away, owing to the strength of the current. When we arrived on the far side, the old woman revealed herself as the goddess Hera.

'I will be at your side in your efforts to oust Pelias,' she said. 'I detest the fellow. He promised to dedicate a shrine to me in Iolcus but he hasn't. Make sure you honour me once you ascend the throne.'

'That's inexcusable,' I commented. 'Once I'm king, you will receive the worship that you deserve as queen of heaven.' Then I looked down at my feet. 'Damn it, I've lost one of my sandals in the river. Oh well, too bad.'

I arrived in Iolcus around teatime and headed immediately to the palace. I introduced myself to Pelias as the long-lost son of his half-brother. I caught him glancing suspiciously at my feet. I later learned he'd been warned by an oracle to be wary of a man wearing one sandal. It didn't take him long to put two and two together.

'What a pleasure to meet you, Jason,' he said with affected warmth. 'Your mother erroneously informed me you were dead. Where have you been all these years? The throne is yours, of course. But I think you should undertake an adventure before you assume the kingship.

It'll help prepare you for the challenges of monarchical rule. Why not head to Colchis and bring back the Golden Fleece? It's currently in the possession of King Aeëtes. I suggest you leave as soon as possible. The sooner you go, the sooner you'll be back and the sooner you become king.'

Pelias waved me away with a flick of the hand. I knew that recovering the Golden Fleece was one of the toughest challenges imaginable. I could hardly refuse, however. I didn't want to look like a wimp. I put out a general call to all the heroes, inviting whoever wished to join me.

The response was amazing. Before long no fewer than forty-nine strapping heroes had signed up. Well, not literally. Most of them couldn't write, so they sent word of their intent to come by means of carrier pigeons. The heavy hitters included Heracles and Philoctetes, both fantastic archers; Orpheus, an amazing singer; the twins Castor and Pollux, otherwise known as the *Dioskouroi*, or Youths of Zeus because Zeus was their father; Telamon, the father of Teucer, who fought at Troy; Peleus, the father of Achilles; and the sons of Boreas, the chill wind that comes out of the north. I won't go on. That's just the cream of the cream. Long story short, it was impressive testimony to the high esteem in which I was held among the heroes.

A craftsman called Argo built a ship with fifty oars to transport us across the Aegean Sea. I called it the *Argo* in his honour. We who sailed in it are known as the 'Argonauts'.

On the way to Colchis [known today as the Crimea], which was where the Golden Fleece was hanging, we stopped off on Lemnos. We were greeted by a beautiful woman with ivory white skin, dimpled cheeks and a unibrow called Hypsipyle, the daughter of Thoas and granddaughter of Dionysus. She was super friendly, but I sensed that something was a bit off. None of the women living on the island was married. In fact there wasn't a man to be seen anywhere. Naturally I was curious to know why.

'Why aren't there any men here?' I asked, tucking into a plate of jugged hare which she had offered me on arrival at her palace.

'It's because of Aphrodite,' she explained. 'We offended her so she punished us by making us smelly. So smelly that none of the men on the island wanted to touch us with a barge pole. Instead they satisfied their lust by sleeping with slave girls, importing them from Thrace. This made the Lemnian women so angry that they massacred all the males they could find in a single night. It was a bloodbath. I was the only one who didn't participate. I couldn't bring myself to kill my father. I put him inside a wooden chest, which I cast out to sea. I'm hoping the chest has washed up somewhere but I haven't heard.'

The fact that the Lemnian women were afflicted with a foul odour didn't trouble the Argonauts one iota. They had a rare old time because the women hadn't seen any men in years. The only one who was impatient to get going was Heracles. Eventually I told my companions to abandon the flesh pots of Lemnos and we sailed off.

The reason why Heracles had no interest in dallying on Lemnos was because he was having an affair with a young fellow called Hylas. When we arrived on Chios, Hylas disappeared. Some nymphs had taken a fancy to him and had dragged him down to their watery bower. Heracles was utterly distraught. He looked for Hylas everywhere, but with no success. I don't know whether you've ever seen a hero cry, but it's not a pretty sight. In the end we continued without him. He never recovered his beloved Hylas, who remains to this day a prisoner in what is surely by now a watery tomb.

We sailed on to Colchis, our oars churning the white manes of the deep. As soon as we docked, I left the lads in the *Argo* and went searching for the palace of King Aeëtes.

'King Pelias of Iolcus has set me the task of securing the Golden Fleece,' I informed Aeëtes. 'Do you have any problem with that?'

'Fair enough,' Aeëtes replied. 'I've never have much use for it. But first you'll have to plough a field with a team of brazen-hoofed oxen and sow dragon's teeth in the furrows. Do we have a deal?'

'Fine,' I replied. 'But I can't quite see the point of the exercise.'

'You will,' he assured me, handing me a bucketful of dragon's teeth, crawling with insects.

The king had a beautiful daughter called Medea. She had watery blue eyes, raven black hair and ruby red lips. She fell head over heels in love the moment she clapped eyes on me. Luckily, she was a witch. She promised to help me perform my tasks on condition that I agreed to marry her and take her back to Greece, which I did. To give the devil her due, which is what she turned out to be, I would never have succeeded in securing the Golden Fleece if it hadn't been for Medea, particularly since the Argonauts proved to be pretty useless.

The moment that I sowed the dragon's teeth in the furrows that I'd ploughed with the brazen-hoofed oxen, a race of armed warriors sprung up from the soil. On Medea's recommendation, I cast a large stone into their midst. The stupid gits immediately began fighting among themselves, which is generally what happens when you throw a stone among armed men who spring up from the ground. Each accused the other of being the one who had cast the first stone. All I had to do was watch them bump one another off. It didn't take long as they were pretty good at it. By the time they were through, there were corpses everywhere.

Hand in hand we headed into a dark forest to look for the Golden Fleece. Once again Medea gave me invaluable help. She revealed that the fleece was guarded by a fire-breathing dragon, which I would be able to subdue with a magic potion.

'Thanks. Nobody thought to mention the fire-breathing dragon,' I said gratefully. 'The only problem is I don't have a magic potion.'

'I do,' she replied, whisking out a rag impregnated with a noxious substance from the folds of her tunic.

Before long we came to a clearing in the forest. The Golden Fleece was hanging from the branch of a tall oak tree. Under the tree was a recumbent dragon. Fortunately it had its back turned to us. I stole up behind it and shook the rag under its nose. The monster instantly slumped on its side and began snoring.

I shimmied up the tree, unfastened the fleece from the branch to which it was attached, jumped down, and tossed it over my shoulder. Medea planted a seductive kiss on my lips. Then we ran to the shore. As soon as we arrived, Medea grabbed hold of her baby brother, Absyrtus, who was throwing pebbles into the sea. I gave orders to my men to hoist the sails of the *Argo* and start rowing with all their might. They turned out to be no better at rowing than they had been in helping me acquire the Golden Fleece. We weren't far from shore when we spied a ship. It quickly began gaining on us. When it was no more than a league behind, we were able to make out Aeëtes standing at the prow. He was shaking his fist at us.

To my horror Medea suddenly produced a meat cleaver from under her skirt, slit Absyrtus' throat and proceeded to dismember him. I was shocked, to put it mildly.

'I never did like him.' she explained, shrugging. 'We might as well put him to a useful purpose.'

Just as Aeëtes' ship drew level, she tossed one of Absyrtus' arms overboard. When the king saw what she had done, he groaned and ordered his men to stop rowing so that he could recover it. Each time his ship began to draw level, Medea tossed another of Absyrtus' body parts overboard and each time Aeëtes stopped.

Eventually the king gave up and ordered his ship to turn around. Mission accomplished. We still had Absyrtus' head left plus one of his feet, which we tossed overboard for good measure.

We continued sailing across the Aegean. When we docked at Crete a giant named Talus started hurling rocks at our ship. Talus was the last survivor of the Age of Bronze. He had a single vein running the length of his entire body. The vein was filled with ichor, a very fine translucent liquid which flows through the bodies of gods. Once again Medea came to the rescue. She tricked Talus into grazing his ankle on a rock. As a result he bled – not quite the right word in the circumstances but you get the general point – to death.

Eventually we arrived back at Iolcus, where I said goodbye to my companions. They hadn't been much use, but we'd done some serious bonding. I promptly went to Pelias's palace, accompanied by Medea.

'Here you are,' I said, presenting him with the Golden Fleece.

'Thanks,' said Pelias, clearly none too happy at my return. 'But I don't intend to give you the throne just yet. I rather like being king. Why don't you go off and undertake another challenge?'

Observing this icy exchange, Medea grasped one of Pelias' daughters by the wrist and led her into a corner of the room.

'Your dad looks a bit peaky,' she whispered to her.

The girl pricked up her ears.

'You're right,' she replied. 'He's been very tired lately. I'm concerned about him.'

'Would you like me to rejuvenate him? I have the magical skills to do that.'

'Wow! Would you?' the girl exclaimed excitedly.

'I'd be delighted,' Medea replied. 'You'll need to chop him up into small pieces and boil the pieces in a bronze cauldron first. I'll take over from there.'

'That sounds a bit tricky,' she commented warily.

'Nothing to worry about. I've done it a thousand times. It never fails.'

So that's how I acquired the throne of Iolcus.

Iolcus became too hot for us after that, however, so we moved to Corinth, where I bought a palace. In my haste to leave, however, I completely forgot my promise to Hera.

After a few years of domestic life I began to tire of Medea. I found her exoticism something of a liability. You can hardly blame me. She was a witch, after all, and a foreign witch at that. I began to cast my eye on Glauce, the daughter of Creon, the king of Corinth.

'I've been thinking, dear,' I said to Medea one day over breakfast, idly twirling a strand of my beard. 'Having a witch from Colchis as your mother is a bit of a liability for our children. What say we divorce and I marry a princess? Then they'll be guaranteed a rosy future. They're young enough to forget you and it'll all be for the best. That said, I'll always be grateful to you from the bottom of my heart.'

Medea pretended to accept the arrangement. She even presented Glauce with a beautiful dress that she had woven out of gold thread. As soon as Glauce put the dress on, however, her flesh began to burn up. She tried to tear it off but it stuck to her. Medea had steeped the fabric in poison. The poison melted her skin and attacked her breathing muscles, causing her to become asphyxiated.

When Glauce's father heard his daughter's screams, he ran to her and clasped her in his arms. Soon his flesh, too, began to melt. They both died in terrible agony.

Medea wasn't done yet in exacting punishment. She pursued our children through the palace and butchered two of them. Her murderous instincts appeased, she fled to Athens in the chariot that belonged to her grandfather, Helios, who turned up to rescue her in the nick of time. After landing in Athens, she travelled to Thebes, where she encountered Heracles. Heracles had been placed under a curse by Hera, which Medea lifted with magic.

I returned to Iolcus and claimed the kingship, but I had lost the support of Hera, who, in addition to feeling slighted, was now infuriated by my treatment of Medea. I was dozing under the stern of the *Argo* when a rotting chunk of its hull dropped off and struck me on the head. I was out for the count.

Atalanta

Good riddance, Jason. Talking about the Argo, I'm one of the Argonauts. My name is Atalanta. I'm a woman, so no one remembers me.

I'm a terrific runner. After we returned from our adventures, I put the word out that I would marry only a man who could outrun me. Lots took up the challenge, even though I made it a condition that if they failed, I would run them through with my spear.

Pathetic suitor after pathetic suitor failed the test and got the chop. Eventually a young man called Hippomenes came forward. Aphrodite had given him three of the golden apples that are guarded by the

Suitors competing with Atalanta, who is way ahead of them.

Hesperides. Whenever I drew ahead, Hippomenes tossed an apple at my feet, so I naturally stopped to pick it up. He won by the skin of his teeth and claimed me as his bride.

Hippomenes only won me by cheating. He wasn't the only cheat in the history of sport, however. Take Pelops, the eponymous founder of the Peloponnese. 'Peloponnese' means 'island of Pelops'. Pelops was the son of Tantalus, who chopped him up into little pieces and dished him up in a stew, which he then served to the gods. Talk about child abuse. He had the insane idea of proving that he could hoodwink the gods and that they wouldn't realise they were eating human flesh. Demeter began tucking into a shoulder bone and immediately rumbled him. The gods were furious and dispatched Tantalus to Tartarus, where he remains to this day and will remain forever.

Pelops was patched up and restored to life with a prosthetic shoulder made out of silver. Not long afterwards he fell in love with Hippodamia, the daughter of Oenomaus, king of Pisa, a city that is close to Olympia. Oenomaus wasn't prepared to let his daughter marry for two very good reasons: the first was that he was having an incestuous relationship with her; the second was that an oracle had informed him that he would be killed by his son-in-law. He therefore challenged all her suitors to a chariot race, warning them that if they lost he'd put them to death (rather like me). Many had tried and failed.

When Pelops arrived at the palace to accept the challenge, his heart sank at the sight of the skulls of failed contestants nailed above the gate of the palace. He persuaded Myrtilus, Oenomaus' horse-trainer, to replace the iron linchpins that attached his chariot wheels to the axle with ones made out of beeswax. He told Myrtilus that he could have a night with Hippodamia as a reward for his support.

Pelops and Oenomaus were neck and neck round the track until the final lap when Oenomaus' wheels suddenly became detached from their axle. The king was thrown out of his chariot and dragged along the ground till his horses ran out of steam. His body was a mass of cuts and bruises, his face barely recognisable.

History does not record whether Hippodamia had a horse in this race, metaphorically speaking, nor how she reacted to her father's death. All that *is* recorded is that she married Pelops, who ascended to the throne of Pisa.

To atone for his crime, Pelops established the Olympic Games in his father-in-law's honour. So the first contest to be held was won by cheating.

Pelops was also a scoundrel. He reneged on his promise to let Myrtilus sleep with his bride. Myrtilus was so furious that he attempted to rape Hippodamia when she was in her bath. Pelops, who happened to be taking an early morning stroll, heard her screams and came running to her rescue. He thrust Myrtilus off her and ran him through with his sword. As he was gasping his last, Myrtilus cursed all the descendants of Pelops. This is the origin of the famous curse of the House of Atreus, which led to Orestes' murder of his mother.

Orestes

I'm the son of Agamemnon and Clytemnestra. My father was the king of Argos. He was also the commander-in-chief of the Greek army that fought at Troy. My mother never forgave him for sacrificing my sister, Iphigenia, at Aulis before the fleet set sail. But I never thought she was capable of murder. It was her lover, Aegisthus, who put her up to it. He'd begun an affair with her immediately after my father left for Troy.

My great-great-grandfather was Tantalus, the monster who dished up his son to the gods. My great-grandfather was Pelops, who won the hand of Hippodamia by killing her father. My grandfather was Atreus, who dished up his nephews to their father.

Atreus married Aerope, the granddaughter of Minos, king of Crete. Aerope had an affair with Atreus' twin brother, Thyestes. One afternoon Atreus came home and discovered the pair in bed together.

Thyestes leapt up and grabbed his *chiton*.

'I'm so sorry, Atreus. I got a sudden chill. I thought I was going to die. My feet were like blocks of ice. Aerope kindly climbed into bed with me to warm them up. Frankly I owe my life to her.'

Atreus decided on the spot to exact a terrible revenge. He was extremely cunning, however. He pretended to accept Thyestes' fulsome apology.

'Nice try,' he said, slapping Thyestes on the back and tweaking his ear affectionately. 'My wife's a good-looking woman. I'm not surprised she caught your eye. Look, we're family. Blood is thicker than water, eh? Let's put this behind us. Why don't you come over to dinner this evening and we'll have a good chuckle?'

Thyestes was completely taken in. He thanked his brother profusely and promised it would never happen again. When he turned up at his house later, Atreus produced a scrumptious casserole.

'My favourite dish,' Thyestes remarked taking his seat at the table, sniffing appreciably.

In no time flat he had finished and was smacking his lips.

'Seconds?' Atreus asked.

'You bet.'

It was while Thyestes was licking the gravy from his plate with a crust of bread that Atreus casually remarked, 'Not bad, eh? I'm glad you found your sons so tasty. I've saved their hands and heads, in case you have a use for them.'

Atreus motioned to a slave, who stepped forward and removed the cover of a silver platter to reveal two pairs of hands and two heads decorously arranged with sprigs of parsley, rosemary, marjoram, Dalmatian sage, and other herbs.

Thyestes staggered to his feet and produced a stream of projectile vomit. Even Helios was horrified and unable to keep to his usual path across the sky. The day dimmed.

Horrific though the crime was, it's difficult to feel much sympathy for Thyestes in view of what he did next. He went to Delphi and asked Apollo how he could seek revenge.

'Atreus is your twin brother,' Apollo informed him. 'You can't kill your twin. That's strictly forbidden. There's only way out of this dilemma. You're going to have to sleep with your daughter, Pelopia.'

'Sleep with my daughter?' Thyestes gasped. 'Isn't that strictly forbidden as well?'

'It's allowable in this one case,' Apollo replied. 'Your son from that union will be the one to avenge you.'

Thyestes departed from the shrine downcast. He was so bent on revenge, however, that he resolved to go through with it. He decided to assault Pelopia at night so that she wouldn't recognise him. He waited behind a bush when she was performing a sacrifice to the Underworld gods and forced herself upon her. As he sought to make his getaway, however, Pelopia grabbed hold of his sword.

Nine months later Pelopia gave birth to my uncle, Aegisthus. She had no intention of rearing an infant who was the product of rape, however, so she exposed it. A few years later, Thyestes was taking a stroll one day when he came across a family of shepherds. A small boy was playing with a dog. Thyestes observed him for some time, struck by the boy's regal appearance.

'Is that your biological son?' he asked at last.

'No, he isn't,' the male shepherd said. 'He was abandoned.'

'I'll give you a good price for him,' Thyestes said.

The shepherds agreed and Thyestes brought the boy up as his son, not realising that he actually *was* his son. When Aegisthus had grown to manhood, Thyestes summoned him.

'I have a favour to ask. I want you to kill my brother, Atreus. He's the king of Mycenae.' Then he caught sight of the sword that Aegisthus was wearing. 'Hang about. Where did you get that from?'

'This?' Aegisthus replied, fingering the scabbard. 'A woman gave it to me. She said it was a family heirloom. Why do you ask?'

'Never mind. Where does the woman live?'

Aegisthus gave him the address and in fear and trembling Thyestes sent his soldiers to fetch her.

'I don't quite know how to say this, dear,' he began when she was led in. 'But I have an awful suspicion that the man standing before us is our biological son and that you are my long-lost daughter, Pelopia. In other words, I'm the man who raped you that night in the sanctuary. Please accept my sincere apologies. Before you fly off the deep end I can explain everything …'

But before Thyestes could get another word out, Pelopia drew the sword out of Aegisthus' scabbard and plunged it into her breast. She fell to the ground, a pool of crimson blood extending outwards around her.

Both Thyestes and Aegisthus gasped in horror. Before Aegisthus could take in fully what he had witnessed, Thyestes extracted the sword from his daughter's breast and handed it to his son.

'As I was saying, I want you to kill your uncle,' he said, doing his best to put a brave face on the situation. 'It's he who caused this mess in the first place. Don't delay. Head to Mycenae straight away.'

Thyestes bundled Aegisthus out of the door. Then he instructed his slaves to remove the body.

When Aegisthus arrived in Mycenae, Atreus was performing a sacrifice. 'That's from my father,' he said, plunging the sword into his uncle's midriff.

Like I said, Aegisthus began his affair with my mother shortly after my father left for Troy. They murdered him the day he returned. Then they packed me off to the centaur Chiron, who ran a profitable business in educating heroes.

It's the duty of a son to avenge his father's murder no matter what. I would never have been able to hold my head up in public if I hadn't. I returned to Argos some ten years later. The first thing I did was to visit my father's grave. My sister, Electra, was pouring libations to appease his spirit, which she did on a daily basis.

At first she refused to believe that I was her brother. The more she examined my features, however, the more she became convinced. Eventually, she fell into my arms and began sobbing.

'You don't know how much I've missed you,' she said, grasping my cheeks in both hands and staring intently into my eyes. 'I've felt so alone. I've had no one to confide in. Not a day has gone by when I haven't dreamt you would return. I can't believe it's really you.'

'It *is* me, Electra, I assure you. Look, we have the same eyes, the same hair colour, and the same size feet. You always had large feet. I'm here to make sure our mother pays for her crime. But we have to act fast. If she discovers I've returned, our goose will be cooked. Let's devise a plan.'

'I already have a plan,' Electra replied. 'Pretend you're a close friend of Orestes. You've come to report his recent death. Say that he died in a chariot race. That'll put her off guard.'

'Brilliant!' I exclaimed excitedly. 'By the way, that man over there is my friend, Pylades. He's vowed to help me. It's not going to be easy. Matricide is a terrible crime, even when it's justified.'

'I know,' agreed Electra. 'And I don't envy you. Let's evoke the spirit of our father before we proceed.'

So we prayed at our father's tomb asking for his succour in the task that lay ahead. Then I headed off to the palace, leaving Electra at the tomb.

It all worked brilliantly. When I announced to the guard that I had news of Orestes, Clytemnestra immediately came out.

'What is it?' she demanded breathlessly.

'I'm afraid I have some bad news for you, madam. Your son, Orestes, has met with a serious accident,' I replied.

'Serious? How serious?'

'He's dead.'

'Dead?' Clytemnestra repeated, the blood draining from her face. 'That's … terrible. How did he die?'

I stared at her. I couldn't be sure if she was relieved to learn of my death or saddened by it.

'Why are you looking at me like that?' she inquired suspiciously.

'I'm sorry,' I said, quickly turning away. 'It's just that the news I'm bearing is so painful for me to report. Your son was my best friend.'

I proceeded to give my mother a detailed account of the race. I described how Orestes was in the lead until he entered the home straight and his chariot overturned.

'Was he in much pain?' she asked, wincing.

'No, he died instantly. He didn't feel a thing.'

Clytemnestra wiped away a tear. Was this for show or was she genuinely moved? She invited me into the palace for refreshment. As soon as I was inside, I drew my sword.

'I'm here to avenge my father, the man you betrayed for that effeminate scoundrel, the man you slaughtered in the bath,' I exclaimed.

My mother fell to her knees and began begging for mercy. She bared her breasts and said pitifully, 'Don't kill me. I implore you. I'm the one who gave birth to you and suckled you.'

I felt my resolve begin to waver. Sensing this, Pylades stepped forward and declared in a commanding voice, 'Remember Apollo, Orestes! You're fulfilling his decree. It's he who has directed you to avenge your father.'

Without a moment's delay, I plunged my sword into my mother's belly. She collapsed on the floor at my feet and expired. Pylades seized my arm and dragged me to my feet.

'Come on,' he said roughly. 'We still have work to do.'

Just then we heard shouting outside the palace. Aegisthus had learned of Orestes' death and wanted to know if the report was true.

As soon as he entered the palace, I grabbed hold of his right arm and locked it around his neck before he had a chance to draw his sword. I dragged him over to my mother's corpse. I wanted him to take in the full horror of the scene. My hold was so tight that he could scarcely breathe. I threw him to the ground and plunged my sword into his neck. Momentarily his eyes locked with mine and then his body went limp.

What happened next is a blank. I felt suddenly very tired. I may even have lost consciousness. When I recovered my senses, I saw the Furies hovering above me. Puss oozed from their mouths, snakes writhed in their hair, and a rasping sound emerged from their mouths.

'What's the matter?' Pylades inquired.

'It's them. Don't you see them?'

'See who?'

'Those creatures over there. What can I do, Pylades? They'll drive me insane!'

'Go to Delphi, Orestes. Seek purification for your crime. You've done something terrible. Only Apollo can cleanse you.'

So that is what I did. I hastened to Delphi. I felt befouled all over. I was an outcast. I didn't seek hospitality along the route. I just kept going.

As soon as I arrived I burst into Apollo's shrine and told him I had carried out his orders. His priestess prepared a sulphur bath for me and conducted rituals on my behalf. All this did nothing to relieve my mental agony, however. I was sliding further and further into a bottomless pit, tormented by guilt.

'What can I do?' I demanded.

'You must go to Athens and undergo a trial,' Apollo informed me.

'A trial? What's a trial?'

'It's a place where you will be judged by a jury of your peers. That's the only way you will find any release. Purification is just the first step. I'll accompany you and be your lawyer.'

'What's a lawyer?'

'You'll see.'

When we arrived in Athens, Apollo led me up onto the Areopagus, or Hill of Ares, which lies to the northwest of the Acropolis. It's called the Hill of Ares because Ares was tried here by a jury after he had killed Poseidon's son, Halirrhothius, who had raped Ares' daughter, Alcippe. Ares had been acquitted of his crime on the grounds of justifiable homicide. I took this as a good sign. Justifiable homicide would be my defence, too.

Athena appointed twelve citizens of Athens to hear my 'case', as she put it. It was the first case ever to be adjudicated by humans. There was a prosecution and a defence. Each spoke, one against me and one for me. The prosecution, the Furies, spoke first. They claimed that no crime was worse than matricide and that if I were to be acquitted, it would send a terrible signal to every other disgruntled son up and down the land.

'You can expect sons to start murdering their mothers right, left and centre,' said Megaera, whose name means jealousy.

'Nonsense,' Apollo replied. 'Orestes's matricide was a special case. He had no alternative but to avenge his father. Besides, mothers aren't as important as fathers biologically. They only provide a receptacle for the sperm. It's the father who generates the active ingredient, so it's the father who's the real parent.'

Well, long story short, when it came time for the jury to vote, which they did by casting ballots secretly, six members 'found' me guilty and six 'found' me innocent. At this point Athena stepped in and said she was going to break the deadlock. She didn't comment on my guilt or innocence. She simply said she favoured males because she was her father's daughter exclusively – you'll recall that she grew to term inside Zeus' head – and was casting her vote for my acquittal. In the future, she decreed, whenever any jury is split down the middle, the accused must be acquitted.

So this is the origin of dockets, briefs, judgements, mentions, arraignments, injunctions, appeals, and all manner of legal manoeuvering.

That wasn't the end of the business, however. When Athena announced her decision, the Furies were – well, in a word – furious.

'You call this justice!' Alecto, Unyielding in Anger, screamed. 'You've humiliated us, Athena. You think you're so high and mighty because you're Zeus' daughter. Well, we've got news for you. We're going to poison this entire land that you love so much. We'll cause a blight to descend over the face of Attica. Nothing will grow. Mothers will become infertile. Crops will become diseased. The groans of the people will rise to the summit of Mount Olympus.'

'Steady on, revered ones,' Athena replied. 'I urge you to show some respect for Zeus. I wouldn't want him to blast you with his thunderbolt. That wouldn't do you much good.'

'Don't you threaten us!' Tisiphone, Avenger of Murder, snarled. 'We're not afraid of Zeus or any of the Olympians. We mean what we say.'

'Let's come to a compromise, ladies,' Athena said gently. 'I acknowledge that you are older than I am and for that reason you deserve my respect. I invite you to take up residence in my land. There's a cave on the north side of the Acropolis. It's yours. All Athenians will fear you. They'll know that if they anger you by committing a crime against a close relative, you will bring them to justice. We'll have to change your name, however. I suggest we call you the Kindly Ones in the future. Is it a deal?'

The newly named Kindly Ones looked at each other.

'Deal,' Megaera said eventually.

After my acquittal I headed back to Argos, where life returned to normal, for which I am grateful.

I always thought I'd had a pretty miserable lot. That was before I heard what Oedipus had to go through. Killing your mother is one thing. Sleeping with your mother is quite another.

Oedipus

My life was a giant testimony to the enormity of human ignorance. Even before I stuck pins in my eyes, I was like a blind man climbing a staircase that led nowhere. Isn't that what we're all doing? None of us knows who we are, and if you want to see that message writ large, just ponder upon the fate of Oedipus.

Mine is the hard luck story to end all hard luck stories. I've tried to make sense of my life, but it's impossible. It's beyond senseless. Only someone with a very sick imagination could have devised it. And who might that person be? Apollo? Surely not. Fate? Who knows? All I do know is that I didn't have any choice in the matter. My life was mapped out before I was born.

When my mother, Jocasta, became pregnant with me, Laius, my father, consulted the Delphic Oracle. It seemed like a reasonable thing to do. I often wonder what would have happened if he hadn't. He was horrified to learn that I was going to kill him and marry my mother.

I can't blame him for what he did next. He merely acted in the way that any sane, responsible father would have done. He couldn't actually kill me for fear of incurring pollution, but he took every step he could to ensure I'd have zero chance of survival. That was why he drove nails through my ankles: to prevent me from being able to crawl. Hence my name, Oedipus, which means 'Swollen Ankle'. My ankles remain swollen to this day.

Fate? What is Fate? Who fixes Fate? Why was it fated that I should kill my father and marry my mother? What purpose did it serve? I've been tearing my brains apart ever since I discovered my true identity and I've never come close to being able to justify either my sufferings or those I unwittingly inflicted on others. Life has no purpose if such things can happen.

When Laius received the oracle, he didn't throw his hands up in despair and say to Jocasta, 'How unfortunate. Well, I suppose we'll have to accept the fact that our baby is going to grow up to commit the worst possible crimes imaginable, so let's just bow our heads to Fate and show him as much love as we would any normal child.' Who would do that? Instead, after piercing my ankles, he handed me over to a servant with instructions to abandon me in the wild.

The servant just couldn't bring himself to do that, however. Instead he handed me over to a nomadic herdsman, who in turn handed me over to Polybus and Merope, the king and queen of Corinth. Polybus and Merope happened to be childless and were delighted to receive a baby boy, even one whose ankles were horribly deformed. It was they who gave me my name.

My adoptive parents never told me that I wasn't their biological child. I therefore grew up in the belief that I would one day ascend the throne as Polybus' heir. One evening, however, a Corinthian aristocrat drunkenly told me that he had always wondered who my true parents were. I grabbed him by the collar and asked him what he meant, but he clammed up and I couldn't get another word out of him.

I couldn't get what he had said out of my mind, so I decided to go to Delphi and seek an answer from Apollo. When I arrived at the sanctuary, there was a long line of petitioners in front of me. Eventually my turn came. As soon as I entered the shrine, the Pythia – that's the priestess who delivers the god's pronouncements – uttered a piercing shriek and burst into laughter.

'You're the man who's going to murder his father and marry his mother!' she shouted, her ominous words bouncing off the surrounding hills.

I fled from the shrine in horror, the dire prophecy ringing in my ears.

I know what you're going to say. You're going to say that I should have said, 'But hang on. Who *are* my father and mother? That's why I'm here.' Well, who thinks straight when they've just been handed a sentence like that? All I could think of doing was making sure I never set eyes on Polybus and Merope ever again.

Instead of heading south back to Corinth, therefore, I headed east. I hadn't gone far when I saw a carriage trundling towards me. As it got closer, I made out an old man inside. He ordered his servants to shove me off the road. I wasn't going to stand for that, so I struck one of them on the head with my staff. The man died instantly. I dispatched a second servant by knocking his legs from under him and breaking his back. Just as I was about to lay into the third, the old man lashed me with his leather whip. In my fury I grabbed hold of the whip, tore it from his feeble grasp, twisted it around his neck, and strangled him. The one surviving servant ran off.

Further down the road I found my path blocked by a winged creature with the head of a woman and the body of a lion. It was asking every passerby a riddle. If the passerby couldn't answer it, the Sphinx – this was what it was called – hurled him to his death.

'What creature goes on four legs in the morning, two in the afternoon, and three in the evening?' the Sphinx asked me, idly scratching its belly.

'That's simple,' I replied. 'A human being. A human being crawls on all fours in the morning of its life, walks on two legs in the afternoon, and leans on a stick in the evening.'

The Sphinx flew off with its tail between its legs. I continued on my way and soon arrived at the city of Thebes. News of my accomplishment had preceded me, so the people welcomed me like a conquering hero.

The Sphinx.

As luck would have it, Jocasta, the queen, had been recently widowed. If I'd been thinking clearly, I would have thought twice before getting involved with a woman who was old enough to be my mother, but I was on a roll and she turned her attention fully onto me, so I did the gentlemanly thing by popping the question. She agreed, we got married a few months later, and I became king of Thebes.

In the fullness of time we had four children: two boys called Polyneices and Eteocles, and two girls called Antigone and Ismene. If you'd seen us, you would have called us the quintessential happily married couple.

One day, however, everything changed. A plague ravaged the land. The crops were blighted, disease spread through the livestock, and humans began dying with blisters all over their bodies. I immediately sent my brother-in-law, Creon, to Delphi to ask Apollo for his advice. When he returned, he told me I had to expel 'the accursed one', meaning the killer of King Laius. In response I set in motion a high-powered investigation to discover the perpetrator of the crime, vowing to pursue the killer with no less vigour 'than if Laius were my own father', as I put it.

Soon after the investigation began, a messenger arrived from Corinth to inform me that Polybus had died. I felt enormous relief. It seemed that the oracle about killing my father was false, since I obviously wasn't responsible for his death: unless he had died of a broken heart because of my departure. Jocasta made me feel even more relieved by telling me of a prophecy that she and Laius had received, stating that their son would one day kill his father and marry his mother.

It would have saved a lot of grief if Jocasta had told me this oracle *before* we got married. Then I might have put two and two together. But I'm equally at fault in not sharing my own pronouncement from Apollo. Anyway, the conclusion we both drew from the report of Polybus' death was that oracles are rubbish and shouldn't be taken seriously.

It was now that the Corinthian messenger revealed that I wasn't actually Polybus' son.

'Then whose son am I?' I inquired.

'I don't know, your majesty,' the man replied. 'All I can tell you is that I got you from a servant attached to the House of Laius. He'd been ordered to abandon you. It was quite by accident that we met up one day. When he asked me if I knew anyone who would like a newborn baby, I immediately thought of Polybus and Merope. They had no heir so

I decided I would do them a favour. When I handed them the baby they were both very grateful and rewarded me handsomely.'

You can pretty much guess the rest. I immediately summoned the Theban servant who had handed the baby over to the Corinthian herdsman. Reluctantly he admitted that he had received it from Laius with instructions to abandon it where wild animals would dispose of it.

'But you disobeyed?'

'I did.'

'Why?'

The servant paused. Eventually he said, 'Out of pity.'

Pity! So pity was the cause of my misery.

The queen – my mother – went off and hanged herself. She'd worked the whole thing out long before the herdsman had finished telling his story. As soon as a servant reported her death to me, I ran to our bedroom, took the pins from the shoulders of the *chiton* she was wearing, and plunged them deep into my eyeballs. Why did I do this? Because I couldn't bear the thought of gazing upon the faces of my children – who were also my brothers and sisters – ever again, or of gazing upon the faces of my parents in Hades.

I left Thebes, accompanied by my daughters, Antigone and Ismene. Towards the end of my life I arrived in Athens. There I received another prophecy from Apollo to the effect that my bones would protect whichever city I was buried in. When my son, Polyneices, learned this, he appealed to me to return to Thebes because he wanted my help. I felt nothing but contempt towards him, however. He had done absolutely nothing for me over the years, and now, learning that I could be of use to him, he wanted to make amends. What a hypocrite! I cursed him and turned my back on him forever.

Instead I requested Athens' king, Theseus, for permission to be buried at Colonus, just outside the city. I told him I would come to the aid of the Athenians in any future war they might wage against Thebes. He was dubious about the benefits of this promise, since relations between Athens and Thebes were harmonious at the time. Nothing lasts forever, however. Friendships fade and enmities arise. It's the same old same old.

Shortly after Theseus had granted my request, a mysterious voice bellowed out, 'It's time to be on our way, Oedipus. We've delayed too long.'

Not even my one surviving daughter Ismene knows where I'm buried.

Ismene

When my father abdicated, my brothers, Polyneices and Eteocles, agreed to rule Thebes alternately each year. They tossed a coin and Eteocles got to rule first. When it came time for him to stand down, however, he flatly refused. He claimed that Thebes needed a stable government and that if they kept switching back and forth the state would collapse.

Polyneices was outraged at the breaking of their solemn agreement. He enlisted the city of Argos and launched an attack on Thebes. Seven commanders, including himself, attacked each of our seven gates. In the ensuing encounter all seven of them were killed. Polyneices and Eteocles died at each other's hands.

Our uncle Creon now became ruler. His first act was to decree that Polyneices' body be flung outside the city and left to rot. This was to be a warning to any would-be insurgent not to stir up more trouble in the aftermath to civil war.

When Antigone informed me that she was going to bury our brother in defiance of this decree, I thought she had gone crazy. Creon was cantankerous and testy at the best of times, and this was hardly the best of times. Besides, his proclamation had a point. He was eager to establish his authority on a firm footing. The civil war had seriously weakened Thebes and he saw it as his responsibility to restore order and stability.

But that wasn't the way my sister saw things. All she could think about was Polyneices' rotting corpse. As if a corpse is the most important thing in the world; more important than life itself!

As soon as the proclamation was issued, she asked whether I would participate in her hare-brained scheme. I was always careful how I addressed my sister. She had a terrible temper and the least thing could set her off.

'I fully understand why you would want to do that,' I replied cautiously. 'But I don't think it's a very good idea. You're bound to get caught and you know what our uncle's like. Why provoke him needlessly?'

113

'Needlessly!' she repeated. 'You think that burying the dead is a needless exercise? I can't believe you just said that, Ismene. And I'll tell you something else. I don't care if I do get caught. I want the world to know how much I love our brother. Now are you with me or not?'

'Please don't put me in this quandary, Antigone. Hasn't there been enough misery in our family already? Just think of our poor father. If he were alive today, he'd surely be advising caution. If he'd been a bit more circumspect, our family wouldn't be in the mess that it is today.'

'Circumspect! You really know how to offend, Ismene. I'll ask you one more time. Do you want to share with me the glory I will earn by honouring our brother's corpse or do you want to pass the rest of your life in ignominy? It's your decision. Polyneices deserves our love and this is the way to prove it. Do you really want his body to be torn apart by beasts and birds?'

'Of course I don't, but that isn't the point.'

'It certainly *is* the point! How on earth will we be able to face our brother in Hades if we don't save his body from that fate?'

'I love Polyneices just as much as you do, Antigone.'

'You're a coward, Ismene. You always have been. Our father would be ashamed of you.'

And with that she stormed off.

Soon afterwards, as I predicted, she was caught in the act by the soldiers whom Creon had appointed to guard the corpse from burial. She'd got away with sprinkling earth over it the first time. That wasn't good enough for her, however. She actually wanted to get caught so that people would know what she had done. So she hid and sprinkled earth over it a second time.

As soon as Antigone was brought before Creon, she began hurling insults at him. She said his proclamation had no force and that she obeyed a higher authority.

'You're just a petty tyrant!' she screamed. 'You can't place yourself above the unwritten laws. They were established from the beginning of time and no one has the right to suspend them. There's nothing more sacred and inviolate than the right of the dead to burial.'

Well, I don't need to tell you what Creon's reaction was to this tirade. Any instinct he might have had to show leniency to his niece went straight out of the window.

'That's enough!' he barked, rising from his throne in intemperate fury. 'I don't need to listen to this. I sentence you to death with immediate effect.'

The moment Antigone's doom was pronounced, the news spread like wildfire throughout Thebes. I ran to the palace.

'Have you come to witness your sister's execution?' Creon taunted me when I burst into the throne room.

'Please, uncle,' I implored, prostrating myself before him. 'Tell me this is just a baseless rumour. You can't condemn your niece to death. She's always been headstrong. We both know that. She'll apologise once she calms down. Rescind the sentence. Or if you won't, condemn me to death as well. I was part of the discussion that led to her decision to disobey your decree.'

You can imagine my surprise when, instead of thanking me for standing beside her, Antigone screamed, 'Keep out of it, Ismene! You had your chance to gain glory when I asked you to join me. But you chose not to do so, so you can't now claim any entitlement to the honour that is mine and mine alone.'

Her reaction took the wind completely out of my sails. There I was, doing her a really big favour, at the risk of my life no less, and all she could think of was her precious honour.

I was about to leave when Creon's son, Haemon, Antigone's fiancé, turned up. He, too, had just heard the news. He was doing his best to mask his feelings but he was trembling visibly.

'What brings you here, my boy?' Creon demanded gruffly. 'I trust you haven't come here to give your father a lecture on statecraft.'

'Of course not, Dad. I respect you too much for that. I'm only here to pass on some words of warning to you.'

'Words of warning?' Creon repeated. 'That sounds suspiciously like you're taking *her* side. Well, let me give you some words of warning, Haemon. Don't ever let yourself be ruled by a woman. If you do, people will play you for an idiot. They'll know you're a pushover and they'll take advantage of you.'

'I understand where you're coming from, Dad, but I have to warn you that the citizens of Thebes aren't taking kindly to your proclamation. There's a lot of mumbling and grumbling going on. Look, forget the fact that Antigone is my fiancée. That's not why I'm here. It's you I'm concerned about. Your welfare. I don't want you putting yourself at risk.'

'And you think that by bowing down to a woman I'll avoid putting myself at risk?' Creon shouted. 'Is that what you're saying? Are you really such a milksop that you know so little about the world? How dare you come here and order me around! What do you know about government? I've half a mind to execute your precious fiancée before your eyes. Maybe that would teach you a lesson. You've got to make hard choices in this world if you want to get on, son. You think that weakness is the way to rule? Guard! Prepare to execute Antigone!'

'Are you serious?' Haemon exploded. 'You sicken me. You'll never set eyes on me again.'

And with that he rushed out of the room.

'Haemon, come back!' Creon roared. 'I haven't given you permission to leave, damn you!' Then he turned to the guards. 'OK, that does it,' he said. 'Take this woman to some deserted spot and immure her inside a rocky tomb. Leave her with just enough food so that she can survive for a few days. That way I can't be held responsible for her death. And do it now!'

No sooner had the guards led Antigone away, than the blind seer, Teiresias, arrived, escorted by a small boy. Creon was all smarmy to begin with and began praising Teiresias for his wisdom and seercraft.

'Best of seers, what an honour it is to receive you,' he said. 'So how can I help you?'

'*You* help *me*, Creon?' Teiresias snorted derisively. 'Do you seriously think there's anything *you* can do for *me*? I'm here to tell you that you have grievously offended the gods and you are standing on the edge of doom.'

'What on earth are you talking about, you old fool?'

'I'm telling you that carrion birds and beasts are polluting our altars with the rotting flesh of Polyneices. As a result the gods no longer accept our sacrifices. You must give the dead their due. If you don't, you will pay such a heavy price that your life won't be worth living.'

'Oh I get it,' Creon snarled, rising in a white fury. 'I know what your little game is. Someone has put you up to this. You're a hireling, that's what you are. A hireling who is blind to everything except money. You prostitute yourself to the highest bidder, like seers the world over.'

This put the cat right among the pigeons. Teiresias, who is also a man not known for the mildness of his disposition, roared back, 'That does it, Creon. I'm not going to mince my words any more.

Your hubris has ruined you. Call yourself a king? You're the lowest of the low. Disaster is about to strike. If you don't recant immediately, you won't be able to save your loved ones from utter destruction.' Then turning to his guide, he said, 'Take me away, boy. I've nothing further to say to this odious man.'

Creon was dumbstruck. He realised that Teiresias was speaking the truth. He gave orders to his soldiers to bury Polyneices and release Antigone from her living tomb, and then he headed after them.

When he arrived at Antigone's stone chamber, he was greeted by the sight of her body dangling from a rope. Haemon had got there just seconds beforehand and was embracing her. As soon as his father entered the chamber, he drew his sword and lunged at him. A soldier just managed to restrain him, so instead he thrust his sword into his belly and expired.

When the news of Haemon's death reached his mother, Eurydice, she, too, took her own life. Creon was devastated. If anyone has been punished for making a bad decision, it's him. And it was all due to his determination to establish his rule on a firm footing.

Well, I did what I could to avert the tragedy. No one can blame me. I think I might go and live on an island. Any island would do, so long as it isn't the one that's inhabited by the Cyclopes.

Polyphemus

The Cyclopes live on an island close to the coast of Sicily. Don't ask me exactly where. I've never ventured to the mainland. We live very simple lives. We aren't consumed with the desire to possess things. Each of us has his own cave. That's all any of us owns, except for our sheep and goats. We make terrific cheeses by the way. You should try them some time, except you can't because we don't export them. There aren't many of us, so there's plenty of everything to go around. We keep our noses out of one another's business, so we don't need laws to keep us in line. We don't bother much with the gods either. Each Cyclops looks after his own family, if he has one. I don't. Sadly I'm a bachelor.

Cyclopes are at heart gentle creatures. We certainly don't go around looking for trouble. We're giants compared with the only other two-legged creatures I've ever seen, those puny little eaters of bread. Though 'seen' is a word that sticks in my throat, owing to the fact that I'm blind. I have to feel my way around now. It was a black day for me when the stranger arrived. But I had my revenge. No one will – I mean No one won't – give me any trouble again. No one isn't his real name. His real name is Odysseus. No one is the name he gave when he introduced himself to me; the lying little sod.

No one and his merry band had barely got enough meat on their scrawny bones to make it worthwhile to tear their wretched limbs apart. I don't normally eat meat, I'm a lacto-vegan, like all Cyclopes, but I did just this one time.

I've no idea where they came from. Puny they might be, but they certainly pulled the wool over my eye. Over my one precious eye, which is now gone for good.

Don't run away with the idea that Cyclopes are stupid, that we're oafish giants without a thought in our heads. Far from it. We're just as intelligent as Mr Smarty-pants and his lot. The little people, damn their eyes.

118

And we're much higher up the food chain than they are. We're divine, you see. Or at least semi-divine, which amounts to much the same thing. Our father is Poseidon, god of the sea.

Poseidon can make tempests that destroy a fleet at the drop of a hat. He competed with Athena to become the top deity of Athens. Their stupid king Cecrops voted for Athena because she promised to make Athens prosperous through the production of olive oil, whereas my dad promised to make Athens lord of the sea.

'Polyphemus' means 'Much talked about,' rather like 'Mr Celebrity'. And I *am* a celebrity, albeit not in the way that I would have wished. It's almost as if Poseidon gave me this name knowing that I'd become famous one day and talked about for generations to come.

Anyway, let me tell you how I got blinded. When I got back from tending my sheep one evening, I found a veritable army of little people sheltering in my cave.

'Who the hell are you?' I bawled. 'Get out of my cave!'

The little people looked as if they were about to mess their pants. Some of them did in fact do just that, as I found out later when I was getting ready to devour them.

The one who called himself No one, however, was completely unphased.

'There's no need for you to throw a tantrum, my good fellow,' he said smoothly. 'We don't intend you any harm. We've just dropped by on our way home. We've been serving under Agamemnon, king of kings, the one whose fame rises up to Mount Olympus. We've just sacked Troy, the greatest city on earth. You've heard of the Trojan War, I presume? Yes? No? Anyway, we're here as your suppliants and all we want is a little bit of hospitality – a gift of some kind, as is customary – and then we'll leave you in peace. Just remember that suppliants are protected by Zeus. You don't want to make an enemy of Zeus. He tends to take the mistreatment of suppliants rather seriously.'

It takes a lot to get my goat but this arrogant little sod did precisely that. I felt like swatting him with the back of my hand, but some evil demon urged me to have some fun at his expense.

'You think I give a damn about Zeus, little man?' I shot back. 'We Cyclopes have no need of the gods. We're protected by Poseidon. And you and your little friends have just signed your own death warrant.'

At that I sprang to my feet and closed the entrance to my cave with a great stone. I grabbed hold of two of the little chaps and squeezed them so tightly that their eyes literally popped out of their sockets. Then I dashed them to the ground so forcefully that their brains spattered the ground. It was the same sort of pleasure you get from killing puppies, if you've ever done that. Then I lit a fire and roasted them on my spit, turning it slowly so that they were well cooked all over. I ate everything: marrow, bones, entrails, guts, gizzards, the lot. They tasted OK. I'm not a carnivore, but when meat comes your way, why not? I washed it all down with a jug of milk and fell promptly asleep.

I slept right through till dawn. As soon as I got up, I milked my sheep and goats, as I do every morning. My chores completed, I seized two more and again feasted on their miniature limbs. Then I headed to the hills with my flocks. Once outside the cave, I took care to put the stone across its mouth so that none of my little prisoners could escape.

When I got back around dusk, I rolled aside the stone and shepherded my flocks back inside the cave. No one immediately rose to his feet and, just as I was about to grab two more of his men for dinner, held out a bowl with a sprig of ivy around the lip.

'Here, try this, big guy. It's called wine. If you had taken pity on us as suppliants, I was going to make a libation to the gods, but since you don't give a toss about the gods, you might as well try it anyway. You look as though you're someone who has anger issues.'

'What are you? Some kind of a shrink?' I replied.

'Just try it. I think you'll like it. It'll calm your nerves,' No one replied.

'I don't have any nerves.'

'Try it anyway. It'll make you look at the world differently. It'll give it a warm glow.'

'Warm glow, my arse,' I replied.

But I tried it anyway, this drink he called wine. Boy, did it taste good.

'Give me some more,' I said.

'With pleasure,' No one replied.

'Tell me your name.'

And that was when he told me he was called No one.

'Well, Mr No one. I'm going to present you with a gift,' I said, feeling my head begin to spin and my speech to slur. 'I'm going to eat all your little friends first and leave you till last. No one will be able to say that I'm not generous, or that I am generous. Or he won't be able to say it. Whatever.'

I must have dropped off after that. The next thing I knew I felt a burning sensation in my eye. No one had taken the branch from an olive tree that I was shaping into a staff. He'd sharpened the end of it into a point and hardened the tip in the fire. It was this that was boring into my single eye.

I thought I was going to die. My eye was literally on fire. The boiling blood was pouring down both cheeks. I let out a howl of pain. Within minutes my fellow Cyclopes were clamouring outside my cave.

'What the hell's going on in there, Polyphemus? You've woken up the whole neighbourhood. It's past midnight. Has anyone hurt you?' one of them shouted.

'No one has hurt me,' I roared back.

'In that case, why are you making that infernal racket? Get some sleep. You'll feel better in the morning.'

And so they all went home.

Throughout the night I heard noises from the little people, but whenever I reached in the direction of where the noise was coming from, I banged my head on the roof of the cave, so in the end I gave up.

I knew it was morning when my sheep and goats started bleating. I let them out of the cave, their udders swaying heavily. I was careful to block

Odysseus and his men blinding Polyphemus.

121

the entrance so that no one could get out – or rather that No one couldn't get out. I felt along the backs of each of the animals to make sure that no one was on their backs. I might be blind but I wasn't dumb. What I didn't realise was that No one had attached each of his men to the underbelly of my sheep and goats. In this way they all escaped.

I didn't realise I'd been tricked until I heard No one taunting me from his ship, which was already heading out to sea.

'Hey, Mr Cyclops,' he shouted. 'You've got your just deserts for eating my men. I'm punishing you for disrespecting Zeus.'

I rushed down to the shore, pausing only to tear off the peak of a mountain that I happened to bang into. With all the force I could muster, I hurled it into the sea in the direction of his voice.

It must have missed him, because the next moment he called out to me again.

'By the way, if anyone comes to visit your smelly island in the future and asks you who it was who blinded you, you can tell him it was Odysseus, son of Laertes, sacker of cities, resident of Ithaca.'

This time I seized a boulder lying on the shore that I'd just stubbed my toe on and hurled it again in the direction of the voice. I like to think

Odysseus escaping from Polyphemus' cave by clinging to the underbelly of a ram.

I scored a bull's eye because I didn't hear any more from him after that, but I can't be absolutely sure.

To be on the safe side, I invoked my father: 'O mighty Poseidon, you who encircle the earth with a great stream of water, if I really am your son and you really are my father, kindly arrange matters so that Odysseus, aka No one, never reaches his home, or if he does reach home, please make sure that he loses all his shipmates along the way and has a miserable homecoming.'

After all this I fell in love with a sea nymph called Galatea. I even wrote love songs to her. She rejected me, however. She told me she was in love with a youth called Acis, the son of some worthless naiad. I was so angry when I heard this that I hurled a rock at Acis next time I heard them canoodling together. It struck him full in the face and buried him in the ground.

At least I take satisfaction for having cooked Odysseus' goose.

Odysseus

I realise now that it wasn't exactly intelligent to reveal my name to the Cyclops. My confounded ego prompted me to do it. I admit I've got a pretty big ego. So would you, if you were me. I'm famous for my trickery and I wanted Polyphemus to mouth off about who had tricked him. That's what his name means: 'Much talking'. My fame, as you probably know, has reached Mount Olympus. That's no mean feat. I know that for a fact because I have the unwavering support of Athena.

But – and it's a rather big 'but' – if I hadn't given the Cyclops my name, he wouldn't have been able to curse me. I wouldn't have had to spend ten years of my life before arriving home. Penelope wouldn't have been plagued by the suitors. My shipmates wouldn't have drowned. I wouldn't have lost all the treasure I took from Troy. I wouldn't have had to disguise myself as a beggar, and so on and so forth. There's a lesson there somewhere. Damned if I know what it is, though.

After we had (barely) escaped from the Cyclops' island, we headed towards the floating island of King Aeolus, the king of the winds. Aeolus received the winds from Zeus' father, Cronus. His island is surrounded by cliffs that rise sheer from the sea. The cliffs are surmounted by a solid bronze wall several cubits high.

Me and my men stayed with Aeolus a full month. He has an odd set up. He has six sons and six daughters, and they're all married. I mean they're married to one another. I've seen a thing or two in my time, but never anything like this. I'm broad-minded, but you have to draw the line somewhere.

At the end of the month Aeolus said to me, 'Look here, Odysseus, the Aegean Sea is unpredictable at the best of times. You'll need this.'

He handed me a bag tied up with a piece of silver string.

'What is it?'

'It's a bag containing the winds. Guard it with your life and use them only when you need to.'

'Got it. Thanks a lot.'

At dawn the next day I bade Aeolus and his lovely wife goodbye. Then I set sail. Once we were safely clear of the harbour, I carefully untied the knot and let only the northwest wind out. It blew our ship safely and smoothly all the way to the island of Ithaca.

The journey took us nine days. On the tenth day a cheer arose from the lads as the outline of the rocky island came into sight. Soon we could even make out some inhabitants on the shoreline. I suddenly felt exhausted. I hadn't slept a wink in days. I lay down on the deck and decided to take a nap. Before I knew it, I was sound asleep.

It was bad timing. As soon as I dropped off, my men started muttering.

'What do you think is in that bag?' asked one.

'I bet it contains treasure,' another replied.

'Why should that lying little sod get all the treasure?' opined a third. 'Haven't we suffered as much as him? We should share it out.'

'Bloody right,' a fourth agreed.

As soon as they untied the knot, the winds flew forth in a rush like air from a balloon. They bore us all the way back to Aeolus' island.

I was furious, with myself as much as with my men. When we docked in the harbour, I disembarked and climbed the steps to Aeolus' palace with a heavy heart. The king was at dinner with his family. He was carving thick slices from a roasted boar and tossing them onto bronze platters for each family member in turn.

'What the heck are you doing back here, Odysseus?' he demanded, interrupting the operation.

I explained how my companions' curiosity had got the better of them.

Aeolus shrugged, 'Sorry, old chap. I'm afraid there's nothing I can do. You must be hated by the gods. I must ask you to leave immediately. I don't want any trouble.'

Aeolus gestured me away with his knife.

I returned to my ships and broke the news to my men. The feebler ones started snivelling.

'It's your own stupid fault,' I told them. 'You shouldn't have opened the bloody bag.'

'And you shouldn't have stayed in the bloody Cyclops' cave,' said one.

'And you shouldn't have fallen asleep,' said another. 'You are our captain after all.'

There was no favourable wind to help us on our way, so we all had to row this time. It was exhausting work. Eventually we arrived at a harbour with two towering promontories on either side. We had no idea where we were. The odd thing about the place was that the sun never set, so it never got dark. I took a couple of my men and decided to explore the island.

We hadn't gone far when we encountered a young girl. I asked her who the people of the island were. She told me they were called Laestrygonians. She pointed me in the direction of a palace. On entering, we were greeted – not exactly the right word in the context – by a mountainous hulk of female flesh. I was about to introduce myself to her when her male equivalent entered, also mountainous, and seized both my companions. He tossed them into a skillet which he seemed to conjure up from nowhere and began roasting them over the hearth.

Oh no, I thought. Not another cannibal. It was *déjà vu* all over again.

I ran back to the harbour and ordered my men to set sail immediately. As we were rowing away, the Laestrygonians started hurling boulders at our ships.

They scored a bull's eye practically every time and only my ship succeeded in escaping. Once it was out of range, I told my companions to stop rowing. I was hoping we might be able to pick up some survivors. No such luck. The Laestrygonians kept launching boulders at us from the cliffs, so there was nothing to do but to head off.

I decided to give my crew a little pep talk. 'Think of the entertaining stories you'll be able to tell your wives and children when you get back to Ithaca,' I said.

They weren't impressed.

A day or so later we arrived at an island called Aeaea. We were so exhausted that we slept on board our ship in the harbour for two full days. On the third day I left my men and went inland to find something to eat. I happened to see a fine stag, which I shot and carried back to the ship.

After we had filled our bellies with its sizzling meat, I said, 'OK, we should divide into two groups. The group on my right will stay here with me. The group on my left will scout out the island.'

There were some protests at the fact that I was staying behind, but I assured them that there was nothing to fear.

When the group of scouters arrived at a modest-sized palace, they left one of their number at the gate and entered the forecourt. It was deserted. The only sign of life was the sound of a woman singing.

'Anybody there?' one of my men called out.

The singing stopped and an attractive woman, no longer in the flush of youth but well-preserved, descended from the upper storey into the forecourt.

'Welcome to my humble abode,' she said with a broad smile. 'My name is Circe. I expect you're hungry. Come inside and I'll give you something to eat. I happen to have some excellent Pramnian wine which I've been keeping for a special occasion. It isn't every day that I have the opportunity to entertain strangers. I live a very quiet life here.'

My men thanked her profusely and followed her into the palace. Circe led them into the dining room and invited them to recline on couches covered with colourful tapestries. Skimpily dressed female slaves laid out a lavish spread.

While they were tucking in, Circe secretly slipped a drug into their wine. It immediately rendered them helpless. Then she produced a magic wand and struck each man on the head. In an instant they were all turned into pigs with snouts and bristles and little curly tails.

'Oink, oink, oink,' they grunted.

When Eurylochus, the man they'd left on guard duty, poked his head inside to see what was going on, he was dumbstruck. He ran back to my ship as fast as his two legs would carry him. He was shaking like a leaf.

'Spit it out, man,' I ordered. 'What's happened?'

'I don't exactly know. One moment I was listening to a woman singing, and the next moment I heard pigs grunting and squealing. I think she has transformed our lads into pigs. I had a funny feeling that one of the pigs sounded just like Elpenor.'

'Pigs, eh?' I said coolly, grasping my sword. 'OK. The rest of you stay here. I'm going to find out what's going on.'

As I got near to the palace, a handsome young man came up to me and said, 'Are you on your way to see Circe? I should warn you that she's turned your companions into pigs.'

'Yes, I know that,' I replied, reluctant to engage in pleasantries with a stranger.

Odysseus' men turned into pigs.

'Steady on, not so fast,' the young man said, grasping me by the arm as I made to head off. 'How are you intending to rescue them?'

'I'll decide when I get there,' I replied.

'Not a good plan. Circe is a witch; a very powerful witch. You're going to have to drug her if you want to overpower her.'

At this the handsome young man tore up a plant by the roots that was growing beside the path. It screeched as he did so, just as if it was alive.

'What is it?' I asked examining it.

'It's moly,' the young man informed me.

'Moly? That's an odd name for a plant.'

'Be that as it may, you'll find it'll come in handy. You should crush it and drop it into Circe's wine when she's not looking. There's another thing.'

'What is it?'

'Don't eat anything Circe offers you.'

'I wasn't planning to,' I replied.

'Just making sure. When she goes to tap you with her wand, take your sword from its scabbard and threaten to kill her. And one more thing.'

'What now?' I demanded, impatient to get on my way.

'She'll ask you to go to bed with her.'

'And?'

'Just do it.'

'Very well, if you insist.'

As the young man departed, I noticed that there were wings attached to his boots. In a flash I realised that my helper was no other than Hermes. If I'd known who he was, I'd have been politer.

Everything went according to plan. I crushed the moly into Circe's drinking bowl to lower her resistance. Just as she was about to tap me on the head with her wand, I grabbed hold of her arm and threatened her with my sword.

'Conduct me to your pig pen,' I said peremptorily.

Circe admitted she was defeated. As instructed, she led me outside. When my men saw me, they all tried to get up onto their hind legs to greet me. Their grunts were deafening. Circe tapped each of them with her wand and they became human again. There was a lot of emotion on all sides.

'No hard feelings, I hope,' she inquired tentatively.

'No, none,' I assured her.

'Why not bring the rest of your companions here? I promise not to pull any more tricks on you.'

'Good idea,' I replied.

When the men I'd left at the ship saw me they were mightily relieved. I told them to accompany me back to the palace.

'Are you crazy?' Eurylochus shouted. 'It's a trap. You must have been bewitched. We'll all be turned into pigs.'

'Shut up, Eurylochus,' I said irritably. 'Circe is in my power.'

I got back to discover that Circe's slaves had bathed my men, anointed them with olive oil, and dressed them in woolly fleeces.

'It's time for bed,' Circe said after we had all eaten our fill.

'Happy to oblige,' I said.

I stayed on Aeaea for a whole year, and a merry old time was had by all. I could have stayed longer but the lads became restless. At breakfast one morning I told Circe we had to be on our way.

'You need to make a detour to Hades,' she said, 'To consult with the blind seer Teiresias. He can give you news about what's been going on in Ithaca during your absence.'

The night before we left, Elpenor got drunk and fell asleep on the roof of the palace. When he heard us stirring the next morning, he forgot he was up on the roof, stumbled off the edge, and broke his neck. We wanted to get to Hades before dark, so we didn't have time to bury him.

Once I arrived at Hades, I saw many monstrous sights that will haunt me till the end of my life. The first person I met after sacrificing a black sheep to the dead was Elpenor. He requested I bury his body when I returned to Circe's island.

'It's no fun walking up and down the banks of the Styx for all eternity,' he explained.

The next person I ran into was my mother, Anticleia. Well, not exactly ran into. That would have been impossible, given the fact that she was insubstantial.

'Why didn't you come back to Ithaca immediately after the war ended?' she asked.

'I kept on encountering monsters,' I replied rather sheepishly.

'Monsters? What sort of monsters?'

'Every sort of monster. You name it. I encountered it. I'm lucky to be here.'

'Lucky to be in Hades?'

'No, lucky to be alive, visiting you in Hades,' I explained. I decided to change the subject. 'What exactly is death?'

'Well, for a start, the sinews no longer hold the bones and the flesh together.'

'What happens to the personality?'

'As soon as the breath of life leaves your flesh and bones, your soul flutters and flies away, just like a dream.'

I would have liked to go on talking with her, but I was on a mission. I was relieved to see that the next person who wanted to chat with me was the blind seer, Teiresias.

'Can you tell me what's been going on in Ithaca during my absence?' I enquired.

'Don't expect a warm welcome,' the seer replied. 'That's assuming you make it home. If you do, you'll be in pretty bad shape. You'll have lost all your companions and your palace will be full of suitors, all eager to marry Penelope.'

'Haven't you got any good news for me?'

'All being well, you'll reach a great age and become prosperous. You'll go on more voyages and die far from the sea. I recommend that you build a cenotaph far inland where people have no knowledge of the sea and that you place an oar on top of it. And remember to appease Poseidon by performing a sacrifice at the cenotaph.'

'So life will get better?'

'Yes, like I said, if you survive your homecoming. Doesn't life always get better?'

'Not in my experience, but I live in hope,' I replied.

'Don't we all,' Teiresias replied, somewhat mournfully.

The next person to approach me was Agamemnon. When he told me he'd been murdered, you could have knocked me down with a feather. It turned out that his wife, Clytemnestra, had been plotting his death ever since the Greek fleet sailed to Troy.

Clytemnestra had her reasons, it turned out. While we were mustering at Aulis on the east coast of Euboea, Artemis had become angry because a pregnant hare that was grazing in her sanctuary had been devoured by a pair of eagles. The eagles symbolised Agamemnon and his brother, Menelaus, and the pregnant hare symbolised the Trojans. That at least was how the goddess viewed the matter. I thought this was a bit of a stretch but you can't argue with a goddess.

Artemis demanded human sacrifice in appeasement. The victim had to be Agamemnon's daughter, Iphigenia.

Initially Agamemnon refused. Eventually, however, the army became restless. He had summoned us to defend his brother's honour because of the abduction of Helen by Paris, and now he was keeping us all hanging around.

We wanted to get the job over as soon as possible. We couldn't have cared less about Helen, but we all owed allegiance to Agamemnon.

The king had no option but to concede to the army's wishes. As a way of getting Clytemnestra to send their daughter to Aulis, he wrote to her explaining that Achilles wanted to marry her. When the girl arrived, he lost no time in leading her to Artemis' altar. One priest strapped her down on top of the altar and another performed the sacrifice.

Immediately a favourable wind started to blow, the army raised a cheer, and we set sail for Troy. It wasn't all plain sailing, however. By some inexplicable miscalculation the fleet ended up in a place called Mysia, some distance to the south of Troy. Agamemnon, who was now eager to dispel the impression that he was dilatory, launched a sudden attack on the nearest city in the region.

'Why the heck are you laying siege to *my* city?' the king, whose name was Telephus, demanded, peering down as our men started scaling his walls.

'Don't try and be clever with me,' Agamemnon replied, looking up. 'You know the answer perfectly well. Give us back Helen or we'll destroy your city, kill all your men, and rape all your women.'

'Who's Helen? I don't know anyone by that name,' Telephus replied.

'Very funny. I'm going to count up to ten. If you haven't released Helen by then, Troy will become a smoking ruin.'

'Troy? Did you say Troy? This isn't Troy. This is Mysia.'

Agamemnon's face dropped.

'What the f***?' he exclaimed.

He was forced to return to Aulis to take his bearings before beginning the whole expedition again.

Meanwhile, back in jolly old Sparta, Clytemnestra began plotting her revenge. When her husband returned ten years later, he did so with Priam's daughter, Cassandra, in tow. Not good. Talk about pouring salt into a gaping wound.

A few words about Cassandra. She was the daughter of King Priam. She was extremely beautiful. She had honey blond hair and a sylph-like figure, if you've ever seen a sylph. Not many people have. She had attracted the eye of Apollo.

'Will you sleep with me?' the god asked her. 'I'll give you anything you want.'

'Make it possible for me to see into the future,' she replied after only a moment's reflection.

As soon as Apollo granted her wish, however, Cassandra promptly turned her back on him. Apollo took his revenge by turning his gift into a curse. The girl would see all the terrible things that were going to happen to the people she loved, but be powerless to save them.

'Welcome home, dear,' Clytemnestra said, giving Agamemnon a peck on the cheek as soon as his chariot drove into the courtyard. 'I'm so glad you made it back in one piece. I've laid out the red carpet for you, as you can see.'

'Won't I offend the gods if I soil it with my grubby feet?' Agamemnon inquired tentatively.

'Of course not, you silly. You deserve to be greeted in style.'

'OK, since you've gone to so much trouble for me,' Agamemnon said, finally descending from his chariot and stepping onto the carpet.

Once the palace doors had closed beside him, Clytemnestra conducted her husband into a small room attached to the hearth that served as a bathroom. A terracotta tub stood in the centre, from which steam arose.

'I think you'll find the temperature to your liking,' she said, dipping her elbow into the water to test it. 'Here, let me help you off with your armour. My word, it is rusty. You won't have any use for that any more. Nor for your sword. I'll take that.'

Agamemnon eased himself out of his breastplate and greaves. He kicked off his sandals and tentatively placed the big toe of his right foot in the water. Then he climbed inside, lay down, splashed the sudsy water all over him, and exhaled deeply.

And then it happened.

No sooner had he closed his eyes when a net dropped down from the ceiling, trapping his limbs in its heavy mesh. Clytemnestra unsheathed his sword from its scabbard and plunged it into his belly; not once, not twice, but three times. His agonised cries rang throughout the palace. Then she grabbed Cassandra by her hair and slaughtered her as well.

'Learn from my example, Odysseus,' Agamemnon said, prodding me repeatedly with his insubstantial forefinger. 'I know you think that your wife, Penelope, would never do anything like that, but you can't be too sure. You've been away a very long time. There's no knowing what she's been getting up to in your absence. Women just aren't to be trusted. You take it from me, old son.'

The next person I saw was Achilles. He had been given a choice of two destinies. His mother, Thetis, had told him that he could either live a short life and achieve eternal glory or die an old man and be entirely forgotten. He chose eternal glory.

He wasn't the man I had known. He had a hangdog expression and his shoulders were hunched. I determined to try to cheer him up.

'Everyone's talking about you, Achilles,' I said brightly. 'Your son, Neoptolemus, is a real chip off the old block. We couldn't have won the war without him. You must be greatly respected among the dead.'

Achilles shook his head sadly. I'd only succeeded in making him more miserable.

'I would rather be the lowest of the low in the land of sunlight than lord of all the dead. Who cares about fame? It's worthless in the end. All that matters is life.'

What could I say? As my dear old father, Laertes, always said, you pays your money and you makes your choice.

The last person I caught sight of was Ajax the Greater. Not to be confused with his inferior counterpart, Ajax the Lesser.

Before I could hail him, Ajax turned around and beetled off in the opposite direction. It was clear he still bore an enormous grudge against me. This was due to the fact that when Achilles died after being shot in the heel by Paris, Agamemnon and Menelaus had held a competition to determine who was worthy of his arms and armour. The two chief contenders were me and Ajax.

As soon as I was declared the winner, Ajax went berserk. He butchered a herd of cattle in the belief that he was slaughtering the army chiefs. When he came to his senses the next morning, he felt so humiliated that he took his own life.

Imagine rancour lasting all eternity. Truly a fate worse than death.

Before heading back to earth, I thought it would be mildly diverting to see the really big criminals who are being eternally punished for their unspeakable crimes against the gods. Sisyphus was the first one I saw. He's condemned to roll a great stone uphill. It always topples over just before he gets it to the top and plunges all the way down to the bottom again. He has to go on repeating the same exercise for all eternity. He killed one of his guests so Zeus is punishing him for violating his sacred law of hospitality.

The next one I saw was Tantalus. He is perpetually tantalised by the sight of grapes above his chin and water below, both just out of reach:

hence his name. He invited the gods to dinner and served up his son, Pelops, in a stew.

Lastly, I saw Ixion. Ixion murdered his father-in-law and was condemned to wander along the pathless ways. He appealed to Zeus to reduce his sentence and Zeus had complied. He'd even allowed him to reside on Olympus. Ixion had become besotted with Hera, however, and one day he exposed himself to her. Hera protested to Zeus, but Zeus was unconvinced. He couldn't believe his guest would do such a stupid thing. In the end, he agreed to manufacture Hera's double to see if Ixion would expose himself again. Ixion fell for the trap and did. He boasted afterwards that he had violated Hera's honour. As punishment for his outrageous crime, he's tied to a perpetually revolving fiery wheel.

I wanted to meet more of the big names who inhabit Tartarus, but I suddenly found myself surrounded by a mass of weak, gibbering, witless dead. Word of my arrival had got out and they had flocked to see me. Icy fear gripped my marrow. I was afraid that Persephone might send the head of the Gorgon Medusa to turn me to stone, so I fled, like a proverbial bat out of Hell, out of Hades.

Once back above ground, I filled my lungs with oxygen to expunge the odour of rank pestiferous vapours, ran helter-skelter to my ship, and shouted to my men to loosen the ropes. Moments later we were speeding across the wine-dark sea, our oars slicing through the water at a rate of knots, the shining foam curling on either side of our hull. When we reached Circe's island we gave Elpenor the burial he had requested.

After various other adventures, which you'll hear about in a moment, I ended up on the island of Ogygia, where I got entangled with a nymph called Calypso. I was entirely subservient to her insatiable sexual demands. It was a miserable existence. Well, that's not quite true. It was pleasant enough to begin with, but it got boring after a while.

When I'd put in about seven years of dutiful service to the nymph, Zeus, at the bidding of Athena, decided it was time I returned to Ithaca. So he sent Hermes to Ogygia to give Calypso her marching orders.

'Time to let Odysseus go. You've had your fun,' Hermes said curtly.

'There's no justice in this world,' Calypso replied peevishly. 'Male gods are always seducing mortals but the moment the sandal is on the other foot, they get jealous. Talk about double standards.'

When Hermes had flown off, Calypso found me moping by the shore, idly chucking pebbles into the water and staring listlessly across the deep.

'What's up?' she inquired.

'I miss my wife.'

'You miss your wife?' she repeated, wide-eyed. 'What's wrong with you, man? Isn't a nymph good enough for you? Surely you're not suggesting that Penelope is sexier than I am?'

'Of course not,' I hastily replied. 'Penelope doesn't come anywhere close. She's a bunch-backed toad by comparison. It's just that I feel guilty about staying here and having so much fun.'

'Guilty? Are you serious? What's guilt got to do with anything? Why in the name of all the infernal and upper deities would you want to spend your days – and nights – with an ageing woman? She's probably got wrinkles by now. And a flabby tummy.'

Calypso ran her fingers through my hair and stroked my manly chest.

'Stay with me, Odysseus,' she purred. 'I'll never age. I'll make you immortal and we can enjoy fantastic sex for all eternity. What red-blooded mortal could refuse such an offer?'

'That *is* a pretty good deal,' I admitted, gently pushing her aside, 'but I'm afraid I'm going to have to turn you down. I've also got a son, you see. I left him when he was a baby and he needs his father. I have a family, in other words. I don't expect you to be able to understand that.'

Calypso shrugged her shoulders and turned away. We never talked again. To her credit, she didn't put any obstacles in my way. She gave me the materials I needed to build a raft and let me get on with it.

She wasn't around to say goodbye when I launched the raft, though I think I detected a diminutive figure standing on the shoreline waving in my direction as I dipped below the horizon.

I drifted for days with no sense of direction. When I ran out of fresh water, I began dehydrating under the unrelenting sun. My tongue stuck to the roof of my mouth, my saliva became sticky, and my vision started to blur.

I was on the point of expiring when a gigantic wave hit my raft broadside, shattering the whole thing to bits. Simultaneously a strong current sucked me under. I fought hard to keep my head above water, but the current kept dragging me down and after a while my strength began to ebb. I was on the point of drowning when, out of the immense blackness of the sea, an unearthly voice called out to me.

'I'm the naiad Leucothea,' the voice said. 'Take this scarf. It will protect you against Poseidon's wrath. Once you're in sight of dry land, cast it away without looking back.'

I grabbed hold of the scarf from the naiad's outstretched arm and escaped from the current, buoyed onwards by a strange power.

I continued swimming in the direction of the setting sun. Just as the light began to fail, I discerned a silhouette of cliffs on the distant horizon. I let go of the scarf and headed towards the coastline. I staggered onto the shore, my feet sinking in the wet sand, till I came to a waterfall cascading down a rock, set among gently arching trees. I fell on my knees and greedily slaked my thirst, after first giving thanks to the spirit that inhabited the water. Then I made myself a bed of leaves and, under the star-filled sky, lulled by the sound of the lapping waves, fell into a deep sleep.

I woke next day to the excited shrieks of young girls. The sun was already high in the sky. One of the girls had thrown a ball made out of a sheep's bladder into the sea and they were all frolicking in the water.

I considered what to do. I knew I looked a perfect fright, my body encrusted in brine. I didn't even have a rag to cover my nakedness. But these enchanting girls were also my ticket home. I broke off a branch and cautiously emerged from the bush I'd been sheltering behind. As soon as they saw me, the girls screamed and ran for safety.

All but one, who courageously stood her ground.

Nausikaä

That would be me. I'm a royal, you see. That's why I stood my ground. Plus I was intrigued, I've got to admit it. He was quite a hulk, even though he was old enough to be my father. The stranger stepped hesitantly towards me. When he was within a few feet, he fell on his knees.

'Are you a human being or a goddess?' he inquired hesitantly.

His chivalry took the wind out of my sails.

'I'm certainly not a goddess,' I replied. 'But thanks all the same.'

'I've never seen anything more beautiful in my entire life,' he said softly. 'You remind me of ... of a sapling I once saw growing on Delos.'

I thought that was a bit pathetic, but I quickly realised, too, that he didn't want to say anything that would alarm me, like telling me I had a great body, which I do by the way.

'A sapling?' I repeated just to make sure I'd heard correctly.

'Yes, a sapling. Willowy, just like you.'

'Well, we can't stand here talking all day,' I said after a slightly awkward pause. 'My girlfriends and I came here to do our laundry. It should be dry by now. You'll need something to wear. Here, take this.'

I tossed him a *chiton* belonging to one of my brothers that had been laid out on the rocks.

'My name is Nausikaä. I'm the daughter of King Alcinoüs. You've arrived on the island of Scheria. It's one of the most beautiful places on earth. Pear trees, pomegranate trees, apple trees and fig trees grow here in abundance. They produce fruit year-round because of the climate. We're the Phaeacians. We live at the ends of the earth. We'll take good care of you. We respect Zeus and the laws of hospitality.'

My girlfriends had begun to creep back and were eyeing the stranger with curiosity.

'Could you ladies give me some space?' the stranger asked.

The girls tittered and withdrew. I averted my gaze while he bathed under the waterfall and slipped on the *chiton*.

'You should meet my parents,' I said once he was clothed. 'They'll help you. They're awfully nice people. It's best we aren't seen together, however. The Phaeacians are given to tittle-tattle. They'll assume we're an item. Before we get close to the town, there's a poplar grove. Wait there so that we can get to the palace ahead of you. Once you've gained admittance to the palace, go straight to my mother. You can't miss her. She'll be sitting by the hearth beside my dad. Her name is Arete. Clasp her by the knees and throw yourself on her mercy.'

I got into my cart, flicked my whip, and the mules trotted off in sprightly fashion. The stranger jogged beside me on his blistered feet. It looked hard going for him. No doubt his body was aching from the buffeting it had received.

When we reached the poplar grove, I signalled to him to stop. I later learned that Athena cast a mist around him to shield him from prying eyes while he made his way through the town.

Eventually he arrived at our palace, set in an expanse of juniper, myrtle and oleander trees. He cautiously entered and made a beeline for my mum. Dad and I were seated on either side of her beside the hearth.

After grasping my mum's knees in supplication, he squatted among the ashes of the hearth.

'I'm a broken man, seeking merely to receive assistance on his way home,' he said humbly, averting his eyes.

Dad gazed at him thoughtfully. 'Rise and sit here beside me, stranger,' he said. 'You look like a man of quality who has fallen on hard times. You'd make a fine son-in-law. What do you think, Nausikaä? Why, you're blushing! This is a good place to live. The gods favour us. They sometimes join our banquets. We had a visit from Poseidon the other day. Have you met him? Are you single, by any chance?'

'Sadly, no.'

'Sadly, no, you haven't met Poseidon? Or sadly no, you aren't single?'

'Well, both.'

'Sadly indeed,' Dad replied, casting a mischievous glance in my direction. 'Oh well, too bad. Tonight you can banquet with us and we'll send you on your way tomorrow. Where did you say you were heading?'

'I didn't. I'm heading to Ithaca.'

'Never heard of it. What's at Ithaca?'

'It's where I live. Or where I did live. I've been away the better part of twenty years.'

'How did you get here? We don't have many visitors.'

'It's a long story.'

'Fire away. There isn't much to do here except tell stories.'

'You've no doubt heard of the Trojan War.'

'The what war?'

'Never mind. Anyway, after this war that we won, I set off home, as one does, laden with spoils. The first place I came to was Ismarus.'

'Ismarus, did you say? Never heard of it.'

'It's inhabited by a people called the Cicones. Me and my men burned their city to the ground and massacred the entire population. As per normal, we spared the women and divided them among ourselves. I wanted to leave immediately, but my men insisted on staying on that evening. It was a fatal decision. While we dallied, a few survivors from the massacre told some of the locals about what had happened, and at dawn the next day we found ourselves facing an attack. I lost six men from each of my ships.'

'Sorry to hear that, but you did start it,' Dad observed tartly. 'What next?'

'After sailing for ten days we came to the land of the Lotus Eaters. They're the most laid-back people in the world. They eat lotuses, as you might expect. It gives them a special buzz. They offered some of the leaves to my men. It had the same effect on them. They didn't want to go home after that. I had to use force to get them back on board. After that we arrived at the island of the Cyclopes.'

'I think I've vaguely heard of the Cyclopes. Are they the chaps with a single eye in their centre of their foreheads?'

'Exactly.'

'I thought they only existed in fairy tales.'

'They're real all right. The one called Polyphemus ate some of my men. I put an end to his tricks by driving a stake into his single eye and blinding him.'

'That can't have pleased him. Next?'

'We came to the island where Aeolus, the king of the winds, lives. We got within sight of home but a storm blew us off course. After that, we met the Laestrygonians, and after that we chanced upon a witch called Circe who turned some of my men into pigs, and after that I visited the Land of the Dead. I'm giving you the short version, you understand.'

'How did you manage to visit the Land of the Dead without dying?'

'It's complicated. Next, we encountered the Sirens, who live on an island and sing songs to enchant sailors. If you hear them, you'll never want to go home again. I told my men to stuff beeswax in their ears and lash me to the mast so that I could hear them singing without drowning. Their song was amazing. I've never heard anything like it.'

'And after that?'

'We had to pass between Scylla and Charybdis. Charybdis is a whirlpool. Scylla is a monster who feeds on sailors. She has ravenous hounds attached to her waist. She seized six of my companions and ate them on the spot.'

'And what about Charybdis?'

'It was a close shave. Next, we landed on Thrinacia, the island that belongs to Helios. Circe had warned us to avoid it, but my men were exhausted and insisted despite my objections. I ordered them not to eat any of Helios' cattle but we were stuck on the island for a whole month waiting for a favourable wind and eventually our provisions ran out. So my men were becoming famished.

Odysseus listening to the Sirens.

'No sooner had I fallen asleep when one of my officers, a total jerk called Eurylochus, sought to undermine my authority. He told my men that there's no worse death than dying by hunger because it goes on for days and days. He said there was only one thing to do. They'd have to kill Helios' cattle. They could hold a big sacrifice to appease him once they returned to Ithaca. He'd be bound to forgive them.

'When I woke up, I was horrified to see the ground strewn with carcasses. There was nothing I could do, however. My companions roasted the cows and gorged themselves for six days. On the seventh day Zeus caused the wind to drop and we hastily clambered on board our ship. We'd only been at sea an hour or two when the sky blackened and a wind from the west began to blow. It cracked our mainstay and split the sail down the centre. Our ship suddenly tilted and sank in a matter of seconds. All my men were drowned. I managed to grab hold of a piece of wreckage. I clung to it for days. On the tenth day the gods brought me to Ogygia.'

'Well, you did fall asleep. Where's Ogygia? Odd name by the way.'

'It's where a naiad called Calypso lives.'

'Was she friendly?'

'Friendly isn't the word. She burned with desire for my body. I became her obsession. Have you ever been the victim of obsessional love, Alcinoüs?'

'It happens all the time,' he replied jokingly.

'Calypso detained me for seven whole years. Eventually she got sick of me bellyaching all the time about wanting to return to Ithaca, so she gave me the tools and the materials to build a raft. As soon as I put to sea, however, Poseidon unleashed a storm to end all storms. I owe my rescue to a sea nymph called Leucothea. That's how I arrived here.'

'And how did you find your way to my palace?'

'I asked a passer-by,' he replied.

I breathed a sigh of relief when he said that. He obviously realised I would have got into trouble if he'd revealed I had befriended a stranger.

'You've certainly met some interesting people in your time,' Dad observed. 'I'm just a teeny bit jealous. Not much happens on Scheria.'

'What do Phaeacians do?' he asked. 'Are you traders? I've never come across any Phaeacians in my wanderings.

'Traders? Gods, no. Our island is self-sufficient. We spend our time taking hot baths, changing our clothes whenever we get a bit sweaty, and dancing.'

'Anyway, that's why I'm eager to get back home. I've had enough adventures to last a lifetime. Do you think you can spare me one of your ships to take me back to Ithaca?'

'Who exactly are you?' Arete asked, speaking for the first time.

'Oh, sorry. Didn't I mention my name? I'm Odysseus, the son of Laertes. I'm a sacker of cities. My fame has reached high Olympus.'

Dad scratched his beard. 'Sorry. I don't think I've heard of you.' Then he added, 'A sacker of cities, you said? I hope you haven't come to sack *my* city.'

'That's funny,' Odysseus replied, affecting to laugh.

'I'll see you get home safely. Phaeacians put a very high price on hospitality.'

Then, turning to one of his heralds, he said, 'Announce to all the Phaeacian lords that they must each give our guest a cauldron and a tripod.'

When the ship that Alcinoüs had assigned to take him back home was fully laden the next morning, I knocked on his bedroom door.

'Don't forget me, Odysseus,' I said. 'You owe your salvation to me.'

'I won't,' he promised. 'I will pray for your happiness always.'

It turned out that we would pay a very heavy price for our kindness to Odysseus. When Poseidon found out that we'd conveyed him back home, he was beside himself with rage. Just as the ship that had taken him to Ithaca was about to dock, he struck it with his trident, turning it to stone. Then he surrounded Scheria with a huge mountain so that no one could get in or out.

Odysseus

I felt entirely cut off from the outside world too. I'd fallen into a deep sleep as soon as the ship set sail. I don't remember a thing about the voyage. When I woke up, I immediately suspected that the Phaeacians had robbed me and thrown me into a dark prison. Once my eyes began to adjust to the darkness, however, I was able to make out a heap of treasure stacked neatly against the far wall of what I now realised was a cave. The treasure was at least equal in value to all the plunder I'd got from Troy and lost along the way.

I felt completely disorientated. It was as if my entire life had been a dream. I remember scratching my head and trying to put two and two together but I just couldn't get the figures to add up.

I rose somewhat unsteadily to my feet and began fumbling my way along the wall of the cave towards a faint light at the far end. When I emerged, I felt a chill in the air and began shivering. I could hear a whisper of waves breaking in a rocky bay. A thick mist covered the entire land.

Within seconds the mist began to clear and a furnace of light broke through the bronze-veined clouds. A flock of gulls took flight and swirled across the sky. In the distance a veil of smoke trailed upwards from the roof of a farmhouse.

Just as I was taking the scene in, I felt a light tap on my shoulder. A tall, handsome shepherd boy was peering down at me. I hadn't heard him approach and immediately prepared to defend myself. When I realised he had no hostile intent, however, I asked, 'Could you please tell me where I am?'

The shepherd boy gave me a quizzical look. 'Are you being serious? This is Ithaca. It's a rugged isle, not fit for horses. How come you don't know?'

'Ah, Ithaca,' I replied, concealing my joy. 'I've heard of it. I was captured by pirates. I managed to jump ship last night and swim ashore.

I'm from Crete. I was sent into exile because I inadvertently killed someone. Well, I'd better be getting along now. I mean, I'd better try and find a way to get back to Crete. Nice meeting you.'

The youth bent over and stroked me affectionately on the cheek. Suddenly I found myself gazing into the eyes of the goddess Athena.

'It would take a smart one to pull the wool over your eyes, Odysseus,' she observed approvingly. 'Never tell the truth when you can get away with a lie, eh? That's why we're so well matched. We're like two peas in a pod. We both delight in tricks and deception. Well, you're going to need all your tricks and deception now. I'm going to disguise you as an old beggar. That way you'll be able to sniff out what's going on in your home. Maybe Penelope has shacked up with one of the suitors.'

'Are you being serious?'

'It's a possibility,' the goddess replied noncommittally. 'How many women do *you* know who would remain faithful for twenty years? Statistically, one in five wives are unfaithful to their husbands within six months.'

'Really?'

'I'm just guessing, but I bet I'm not far off the mark. What about you? Were you completely faithful to Penelope?

'No comment.'

'All right, I won't press you for an answer. Let's get going.'

Athena tapped me on the head with her wand and I suddenly felt very old. My limbs became withered, my legs emaciated, my hair turned grey, and I was covered in a foul tunic made of coarse rags tied together with hemp rope.

Penelope

It's ten years since my husband left for Troy and another ten since Troy fell. I don't know any woman who would have remained faithful that long. I can't hold out much longer. I've been rejecting offers of marriage from scores of suitors: 108 to be precise. They've moved into the house and are treating it as their own property. Many of them are sleeping with my slave girls.

I managed to head them off for the past four years by promising to marry one of them as soon as I'd finished weaving my father-in-law's funeral shroud. Every day I diligently worked on the shroud and at night I surreptitiously unpicked the stitches. None of the suitors bothered to examine what I was doing. If they'd had, they'd have rumbled me long ago. Men, I tell you. But now the game is up and I've got to marry one of them. And they're all creeps. Odysseus is – or at least was – the wealthiest man on Ithaca but we're being eaten out of house and home.

Over the years lots of travellers have turned up, claiming they had news of Odysseus. To begin with, I was totally naïve and got excited at the prospect of his return. But invariably the rumour proved false. Each time I received a report of his imminent arrival, my spirits lifted, and when it proved unfounded, as it invariably did, I fell into a dark depression.

My father-in-law, Laertes, is still alive, but he never leaves his allotment these days. He's become a recluse. In the early years we used to reminisce about Odysseus, but after his wife Anticleia died, that stopped. I haven't seen him in months. He lives in a hut on the edge of our estate, tending his vines. I doubt he'll last much longer.

The only bright spot in my life is that our son, Telemachus, is growing up into a fine young man. The other day I was telling our resident bard, Phemius, not to sing one of his mournful songs about the Trojan War because they always upset me.

'I'm the head of the household now, mother,' Telemachus snapped. 'It's not for you to give orders around here. Go to your room and get on with your weaving.'

You can imagine how hurtful I found his words. I didn't want to create a scene in front of the suitors, however, so I did as he bid. Once I was alone, I began to think differently about the incident. Telemachus was making the point that he was ready to take on his father's role and warning the suitors that they had better watch their step from now on.

A few days after this he disappeared. I later found out that he had sailed to the mainland for news of his father. He never told me he was leaving. He knew that if he did, I would try to prevent him and he wanted to avoid a scene. He's growing up fast.

I'm trying my best to keep my anxiety at bay. Telemachus has never been away from home before. At least he's in the company of an adult, a fellow called Mentor, who turned up at our palace last week. I have a suspicion that Mentor is behind Telemachus' decision to go and find news of his father. I saw the two of them deep in conversation.

Even so, it's hard to accept that my little boy is a fully grown man!

Telemachus

Mentor made it plain to me that it was time I did something. I felt a deep sense of shame when he asked me if I'd done anything to find out what had happened to my father, because I hadn't.

Telemachus.

Under his guidance I called an assembly of all the citizens. When everyone was seated, Aegyptius, the most senior member, asked who had summoned it. Then he gave me the sceptre.

My knees were literally wobbling as I stood up. I described how my mother was being harassed by the suitors and how they had moved into the palace and were wasting all my inheritance with their banqueting and rioting.

'My father was a good man,' I declared. 'You all know that. He was always generous and kind. Why doesn't someone put a stop to all this? It's a disgrace!'

By this point I was in tears. I threw down the sceptre and sat down. One of the suitors, a right smarmy bastard called Antinoüs, got up and said that I should calm down, because he and the others had only my mother's best interests at heart. They wanted to protect her and the only way they could do that was if she would agree to marry one of them.

I rose to my feet again and told Antinoüs in no uncertain terms what I thought of him. I called him a freebooter and a thief and I said that if he or any of the suitors had an ounce of decency in them, they would depart today and leave my mother alone. I knew I was talking to a mudbrick wall, but at least I alerted the Ithacans to my plight.

The next day I sailed to the mainland. I knew that the best people to consult were the military chiefs. So I sailed first to sandy Pylos. That's a city at the southwest tip of the Peloponnese, where King Nestor, lord of horses, lives. Nestor was the oldest of the Greeks serving at Troy. Like all old people, he's always banging on about the fact that men today aren't like what they were in his day. He's a decent sort, but he does go on and on. And on.

'No one lives forever, sonny,' he said. 'We all die. Only the gods are immortal. But they can't protect the ones they love. Eventually death catches up with us all. It's the human condition. Nothing we can do about it. We all end up in the same boat. So it goes.'

The old man is highly respected, so I was careful not to display any irritation or impatience.

'I'm sorry I can't be more helpful,' he said at the end of his long speech about life's manifold uncertainties. 'Why don't you try Menelaus? He may have some news about your father.'

Nestor was kind enough to lend me a chariot and two horses and I headed on to Sparta, where Menelaus lives. He was hosting a wedding

Horsemen exercising in sandy Pylos.

party but he invited me into his palace all the same. Before I introduced myself, he started talking about the Trojan War and my father's name came up. I was on the point of bursting into tears when his wife, Helen, entered. She took my breath away. She might have been in her thirties, but she still looked amazing.

As soon as she saw me, she said, 'I'd recognise you anywhere, Telemachus. You're the spitting image of your father.'

Then she turned to Menelaus and said, 'Call yourself a host, dear? Why haven't you offered this young man a drink? Where are your manners?'

Menelaus immediately sprung to attention and summoned a slave. One arrived with a mixing bowl and Helen slipped something into our beakers. Menelaus started to protest but Helen silenced him with a saucy wag of her finger.

'It's just a relaxant,' she said.

Whatever she put into my drink, it felt very pleasant. She then proceeded to reminisce about the last days of the war. I'd heard the story

150

of the Wooden Horse many times before, but she told it in a way that made it come alive. She said the night the Trojans dragged the horse into the city, she was wandering through the streets. My father and about twenty other Greeks were hidden inside its hollow belly. She rapped on the belly and called out to my father by name. It could have cost them all their lives.

'It was a god that made me do this,' she explained. 'I didn't do it of my own freewill.'

'Quite right, dear,' Menelaus chimed in. 'You're entirely innocent. One of the gods who favoured the Trojans got into your head. Lucky for us that this god, whoever he was, didn't succeed.'

It suddenly struck me that Menelaus was afraid of his wife. After all that Helen had put him through, making him the most famous cuckold of all time, and then causing his brother to launch a military campaign for her recovery that led to the deaths of tens of thousands of Greeks and Trojans, she might have felt just a *little* remorse. Not a bit of it. Menelaus danced to her tune and lived in fear of her. In short, it was Helen who wore the pants.

Despite this, I really liked her. She's extremely charismatic. I got the impression that she was still up for an adventure, given half a chance.

'Do you have any news of my father?' I asked Menelaus.

'Actually I do. On my way back home I got stranded in Egypt. It was there that I encountered the Old Man of the Sea, otherwise known as Proteus, who knows all things, or at least most things. As you probably know, he can assume a variety of shapes [hence the adjective 'protean']. Fortunately, his daughter, Eidothea, told me how to capture him. She gave me a foul-smelling sealskin and told me and three of my men to lie down on the beach beside a pod of seals. When Proteus emerged from the water and began slowly counting his seals, we jumped up and grabbed hold of him. He assumed the form of a lion, and then a snake, and then a leopard. He even transformed himself into water but we held him tight.

"What do you want?" he gasped.

"I'm stuck here in Egypt. How do I get home?" I asked.

"Have you tried sacrificing a hundred cows to the deathless gods?" he replied.

"No."

"Well, you should."

'And that's precisely what I did and how I got home.'

'This is all fascinating, Menelaus,' I said, 'but can you give me any news about my father?'

'The last I heard he was having a fine old time on Ogygia.'

'Ogygia? Where's Ogygia?'

'Can't help you there, son.'

Although it had been a pretty useless journey, at least I'd proven I could handle myself in exacting social situations. I left Sparta the next morning and returned to Pylos. Nestor wanted me to stay with him again, but I was eager to return to Ithaca. I'd had enough of windbags to last me a lifetime. I returned home to be greeted by my father's nurse, Eurycleia.

Eurycleia

Odysseus was such a beautiful baby. Like many wet nurses, I spent at least as much time with him as his mother. If only she had listened to me, she'd be alive today. I always told her he would return one day.

I was the first to recognise Odysseus, after his faithful dog, Argos. Of course he'd revealed himself to Telemachus. That must have been a very touching moment; father and son reunited after twenty years. Telemachus was the only person he trusted. He didn't even trust Penelope. That's why he disguised himself as an old beggar.

His cover was almost immediately blown when he first entered the palace courtyard. Argos recognised him immediately. The animal could hardly stand on all four paws any longer. It used to lie on a pile of dung, flicking its tail to keep away the horseflies. As soon as it saw its master, it pricked up its ears, barked hoarsely, and tried to rise up on its spindly old legs. Odysseus completely ignored it. He had to, even though it broke his heart to do so. He knew that if he showed any sign of recognition, the suitors would ask questions and before long they would work out who he was.

So he turned his back on Argos and said with contempt, 'Why is that mangy old dog allowed into the courtyard? It's a health hazard.'

Whereupon Argos whimpered feebly and expired. If that isn't a sad story, I don't know what is.

When Odysseus reached the entrance to the palace, one of the suitors put out his foot to block his path.

'Where do you think you're going?' he demanded in surly fashion.

'I was hoping I might beg for some scraps,' Odysseus replied, affecting an air of humility.

'You'll have to ask that fellow over there,' the suitor replied, pointing to a scrofulous middle-aged man named Irus, who was sitting on a step beside the kitchen. Irus was licking the contents of a bowl, listening attentively.

'Clear off, before I make mincemeat of you,' Irus snarled, without looking up from his licking.

'I didn't quite hear what you said,' Odysseus replied mildly. 'Would you mind repeating that?'

The beggar stopped licking and squinted upwards. A trickle of gravy dribbled out of the side of his mouth.

'Do you want me to knock your block off?' he said.

'I'd like nothing better than for you to give it a try,' Odysseus replied, grasping the fellow by the collar and dragging him to his feet.

Irus was a mean-spirited rascal. He wasn't about to give place to another beggar without putting up a fight and that's exactly what took place. Very soon a number of suitors had gathered around, all eager to witness a vicious fight for the scraps that fell from their table.

The stranger looked like a pushover. Once he stripped off his cloak, however, you could see how powerfully he was built. He knocked Irus to the ground, seized hold of one of his legs, and flung him against the wall of the palace.

After the fight was over, I bathed the stranger's legs. It was then that I realised who he was. I recognised him by the scar on his left leg. He'd got it as a young man when hunting a boar. As soon as I saw it, I knocked over the bronze bowl containing the hot water, making it clatter. Odysseus grabbed me by the throat and gave me a look as if to say, 'Don't you dare say who I am to anyone.'

Of course, I obeyed. I loved my master and I wouldn't do anything to harm him. I'd been waiting for this day for twenty years.

Odysseus now schemed with Telemachus how to kill the suitors. They had help from Athena, who prompted Penelope to inform the suitors that she would marry the one who could string Odysseus' bow and shoot an arrow through a row of twelve axes.

Telemachus and Odysseus' faithful swineherd, Eumaeus, set the axes in a straight line. Then Telemachus picked up his father's bow. He bent the bow and placed all his weight upon it, straining with all his might. He couldn't do it the first time or the second time or the third, but on the fourth go he would have succeeded when I saw, out of the corner of my eye, Odysseus give a slight shake to his head.

'OK,' Telemachus said. 'I'm beaten. Let's see if any of you suitors can do it.'

They all tried but each of them was as useless as the other. Odysseus now stepped forward and said, 'Mind if I have a go?'

'How dare you claim to be on the same footing as us!' the smarmy suitor Antinoüs bellowed. 'No way will you try!'

He was about to give my father a clip on the ear when Odysseus seized his arm and twisted it so hard that he cried out in pain.

He then grasped the bow and strung it effortlessly. He and Telemachus proceeded to rain down arrows on the suitors. Soon there was blood everywhere. Once they had slain all of them, Telemachus told me to round up the female slaves who had slept with the suitors. Then he ordered them to carry out the bodies of their erstwhile lovers. Once done they had to scrub the floor. It took them hours.

Telemachus got hold of a coil of rope, which he fashioned into a series of nooses. He lashed one end of the rope to an outhouse and the other to a tall column in the courtyard. He told the women to place their heads inside the nooses. As he tightened the rope above the ground, he cursed them for being sluts. I tried to avert my gaze from the horrific scene, but I couldn't. It was like watching doves flutter their wings at the instant before they took flight, except that these women weren't flying anywhere.

'Go and tell Penelope that her husband has returned,' Odysseus said to me.

I hastened upstairs as fast as I could on my old legs, panting when I got to the top. Penelope was lying on her bed with an icepack over her eyes.

'Mistress, the day you've been waiting for has come. Odysseus is here. He was disguised as that beggar. Come and see!'

I was expecting her to get up immediately and run downstairs, but she barely reacted.

'You must be very stupid to be taken in by this latest trick, Eurycleia. The gods have clearly befuddled your wits. Kindly leave me alone. I've got a splitting headache.'

'But, it's true, mistress, I swear it! I saw his scar. I know it's Odysseus!'

At this Penelope sat up and looked me full in the eye.

'I still don't believe it,' she said. 'I've been duped so many times. I'm sure he's yet another trickster.'

'Well, he's just slaughtered all the suitors.'

'Anyone could do that,' Penelope remarked offhandedly. 'That doesn't prove anything. Oh well, I suppose I'd better come down.'

My mistress piled her hair on top of her head and secured it in place with a bronze pin. She dabbed her face with white paste so as to appear regal and slipped on her sandals. Then she descended the stairs.

Odysseus was standing at the foot. 'Penelope!' he cried, advancing to embrace her.

My mistress froze. 'Don't touch me!' she ordered.

'Don't you recognise me, dear? Have I changed that much? I know I've been in the wars and the sea has weathered me. I can't help that. But look me in the eyes and you'll see it's me. You don't look a day older yourself. You're still a handsome woman. No wonder all those suitors have been banging on your door.'

Penelope stared hard at him. I could tell she was coming around to believing that he might indeed be her husband. She was fighting inwardly with her emotions, reluctant to yield in case he was just one more charlatan to add to the many who had deceived her over the years.

'You ... really are Odysseus?' she inquired hesitantly.

'The one and only.'

'I'm sorry, my dear, I've had to be so careful over the years.'

'Don't apologise, my love. I completely understand.'

Penelope held out her hand for him to take. 'Let's so upstairs so that we can be alone. You'll see that I've kept things exactly as they were when you left. I haven't changed anything. Apart from the bed, which I've moved from the window. I wanted more privacy.'

As soon as she said this, Odysseus' eyes blazed with fury and he withdrew his hand.

'You moved the bed!' he yelled. 'How in the name of the Heavenly Twins could you move the bed? One of its legs was the trunk of a live olive tree. If you've moved the bed, some man must have had access to your bedroom, and that, as we both know, can mean only one thing.' His voice now went icy cold. 'So tell me, Penelope. Who is this man? I'll wring his neck and then I'll wring yours. You're an abomination. I never thought that you of all people would be unfaithful to me. Agamemnon was right. He told me not to trust you.'

Penelope began crying. 'No,' she said softly. 'Agamemnon wasn't right, if that's what he claimed. I was testing you. Only you could know that the bed was rooted to the earth. I've never been unfaithful to you,

Odysseus. No man has ever entered our bedroom. Have you ever been unfaithful to me?'

My master was about to answer but she gently laid her finger on his lips. Clearly she knew better than to raise the thorny issue of oppressive gender roles at their reunion.

'I don't want to know, not now at any rate. I thought it was you when you came here disguised as a beggar. But I couldn't be sure. I've been deceived so many times. That's why I had to set you a test which only you could pass.'

Penelope took Odysseus by the hand and led him upstairs.

'So, what do you think of Telemachus?' she asked. 'Are you proud of our son? Do you know that he went to the mainland to see if he could discover any news of you? You mentioned Agamemnon a moment ago. Did he get home safely? And what about his son, Orestes? He's a few years older than Telemachus, if I remember correctly. And Achilles' son, Neoptolemus? How did he do?'

Neoptolemus

I was living on the island of Skyros when Odysseus came looking for me. The Greeks had captured the Trojan seer Helenus and he'd told them that one of the conditions they needed to fulfil in order to win the war was to get me to serve in their army. Another condition was that they needed to acquire the poisoned arrows of Heracles.

'That's where you come in,' Odysseus told me.

'What do you mean?'

'Heracles' bow and arrow are currently in the possession of Poeas' son, Philoctetes. You can help me gain his trust. The sod won't give them up easily. He was bitten in the foot by a snake on the voyage to Troy. His foot smelt so bad that I persuaded Agamemnon to abandon him on Lemnos. That's why he hates me so much. But he's also desperate for company and he'll be pleased to see a human face. Just don't tell him you're fighting on our side. Say you've been on a mission to get news of your father. Offer to take him back home to Thessaly, and then, once he's aboard, voilà.'

I agreed to do what he said. I wanted to make myself useful, you see. We landed on Lemnos and I made contact with Philoctetes. I was shocked by his condition. His beard was bedraggled, his eyes sunken into dark hollows, and he could barely drag himself around.

'Why have you come here?' he asked.

'I'm returning from Troy. I was eager to hear news of my father. I'm heading back to the mainland. Would you like to sail with me? I could drop you off in Thessaly.'

Philoctetes was ecstatic. I helped him to his feet and he hobbled on one leg down to the shore, resting his weight on my shoulders.

'Do you mind holding onto my bow?' he asked as we got to the gangplank.

As soon as we boarded the ship, Odysseus emerged from the hold and grabbed the bow from me.

Philoctetes lunged at him helplessly and fell onto the deck. He let out a piercing scream, clutching his foot.

'Damn you both!' he cried.

I felt bad but it was for the greater good. Once we got to Troy, Agamemnon persuaded Philoctetes to use his bow and arrows and it was with his help that we were finally able to take Troy.

The greater good. That's why I helped Odysseus. And that's why Agamemnon had to sacrifice his daughter to get a favourable wind to blow to Troy. And why thousands had to become food for dogs and birds.

War is terrible at the best of times and the Trojan War was as bad as any. Much of the heavy lifting at the end was laid at my door. It was I who killed King Priam while he was seeking refuge at the altar of Athena; I who threw Hector's infant son, Astyanax, from the walls of Troy; and I who, at the insistence of my father, sacrificed Priam's daughter, Polyxena, as an offering over his grave.

For those with a taste for symmetry, the war began with the sacrifice of a virgin princess to the goddess Artemis by her father and ended with the sacrifice of a virgin princess to the hero Achilles by his son.

I hope Odysseus spoke of my exploits when he visited my dad down in Hades.

Neoptolemus sacrificing Polyxena over the grave of Achilles.

Achilles

My mother did all she could to prevent me from going to Troy. She knew I would die young on the killing fields if I did. That's why she packed me off to Lycomedes, king of Skyros. She hoped I'd sit out the war on Skyros. She got me to dress as a girl. It was humiliating. None of the other heroes was playing with dolls.

It was inevitable that I'd be found out eventually. Agamemnon had received a prophecy that my service in the army was essential to the success of his campaign. Three years into the war the trickster Odysseus turned up. He'd been scouring the Aegean for me.

He arrived at the palace disguised as a trader. He had baskets full of trinkets – bracelets, necklaces, rings, anklets and the like – which he flashed in front of Lycomedes' daughters. I pretended to show interest. But then he produced a crate of gleaming bronze swords and daggers and I just couldn't conceal my enthusiasm. As soon as I made to grasp one with a jewel- studded hilt, Odysseus tore away my veil. My cover was blown and I had to go to Troy.

I never liked Agamemnon. I found him arrogant and overbearing. He didn't give a damn about his army. All he cared about was the family honour. So many thousands of Greeks and Trojans died for his family's precious honour.

We were bound to have a falling out sooner or later. And what a falling out it was. That's what led to the death of my dearest friend, Patroclus. It could so easily have been avoided. Agamemnon was so insecure. He couldn't bear criticism. Whichever way you look at it, I was right to stand up to him. Whether it was the right thing to do in the circumstances, well, that's another matter altogether. To this day, or whatever it is down here in Hades that counts for a day, I haven't stopped regretting my decision.

Here's what happened. In the tenth year of the war the army was inflicted with a terrible plague. Men were dying like flies in terrible agony.

It was clear that Apollo, the god of plagues, was angry. So I called an assembly to find out what to do.

'Who knows how to appease Apollo?' I demanded when the entire army had been mustered.

The seer Calchas rose. I handed him the sceptre.

'I can tell you what to do, but you must promise to give me protection, Achilles, because what I'm about to say is going to anger our commander-in-chief.'

'I won't let anyone harm you,' I assured him.

'Well, the reason why Apollo is angry is because Agamemnon refuses to return his comfort woman, Chryseïs, to her father. Her father is Apollo's priest so Apollo is taking it as a personal insult.'

Agamemnon stepped forward and angrily snatched the sceptre from Calchas' grasp.

'Damn you, Calchas!' he shouted. 'I see through you. You've always had it in for me. You're always prophesying things that oppose my interests. It gives you some sort of sick pleasure. I happen to like Chryseïs more than my own wife, Clytemnestra!'

Whoops! His words hung in the air and an eerie silence ensued. He suddenly realised he'd gone too far.

'That said, I don't want this wretched plague to continue,' Agamemnon went on hastily. 'I care for my men. I really do. You all know that. So I'm prepared to give her up. For the good of the army. You'll have to compensate me, however. All these other chiefs here have got comfort women as prizes. I'll be the only one going without and that's just not fair. It's worse than unfair. It's insulting.'

'But we've already distributed all the women,' I protested. 'That's the way we do things after capturing one of the towns surrounding Troy. There aren't any more available at the moment. You'll have to wait till we capture some more.'

'I'll have to wait?' Agamemnon replied scornfully, turning his eyes on me. 'I'll do no such thing. One of you will have to give up *your* girl. Perhaps Odysseus will have to give up his, or Ajax will, or you will, Achilles. I haven't decided yet.'

When I heard this, I lost it. I'd fought so hard and here was Agamemnon calmly proposing to deprive one of his crack warriors of his honour. What's the point of fighting if you don't get rewarded for your efforts?

You have to understand that it isn't just a mere girl we're talking about here. It's the honour that goes with her. When a distribution of prizes takes place after the fall of a town, each warrior is rewarded according to his desserts. I obviously deserved the best prize because, quite frankly, I'm the best of the Greeks. The fact is, however, Agamemnon *always* took the best for himself. So there was a history of bad blood between us.

'You're a totally useless commander, Agamemnon,' I bawled. 'You're cowardly and greedy and you always leave the lion's share of the fighting to me. And now you're proposing to rob me of the little I get for my labour.'

'How dare you speak to me like that, Achilles!' he replied, his face distorted with rage. 'You count for nothing in my book. As far as I'm concerned, you can sail back home to Greece tomorrow, along with those useless Myrmidons who serve under you. I don't need their services, or yours. Meanwhile, I'm taking your girl, Briseïs. I'll teach you how much more powerful and important I am than you. It'll also be a warning to anyone else who might take it into his head to challenge my authority.'

Agamemnon glared at me and spat on the ground. My hand immediately went to the hilt of my sword. I was about to draw it and plunge it into his big fat belly when I felt someone tugging my hair. I spun around and found myself looking into the eyes of Athena. No one else could see her except me.

'I've come down from Olympus at the bidding of Hera,' she said. 'She doesn't want this argument to result in bloodshed. She loves both of you. Lay aside your anger, Achilles. It's not in your best interests to kill Agamemnon. Zeus will make sure that he pays big time for insulting you.'

I stayed my hand, but not without hurling more insults at Agamemnon.

'You drunken, sneaky, cowardly, worthless individual! You'll see what it means to disparage me. I'll get honour from Zeus. You've no idea how badly you've screwed up here today. You'll live to regret what you said in this assembly for the rest of your life.'

And with that I stormed off. I'm a very emotional person and I was having difficulty in fighting back my tears. I didn't want Agamemnon to have the satisfaction of seeing me upset. I needed to talk to my mother.

Thetis

This was the prophecy: Achilles could either live a long life and be forgotten or live a short life and be remembered for ever. We're talking about him to this day, aren't we? So you can work out which he chose. But what mother would have wanted her son to live a short life?

It's my fault. I had tried to protect him by bathing him in the waters of the Styx, the river you have to cross in order to reach Hades, whose water renders humans invulnerable. I'd held him by the heel, however, so I'd failed to immerse him fully in the water.

He visited me on the seashore after his quarrel with Agamemnon. I emerged from the sea and sat beside him. I'd never seen him so upset. He was weeping. I got him to lay his head against my shoulder and I stroked him, just as I'd done when he was a child.

'What's the matter, darling?' I asked.

I knew exactly what the matter was, of course. I also knew the day of his death was now fixed and that he had less than a year to live.

'I need you to call in a favour from Zeus,' he said. 'Agamemnon has insulted me. He's taken Briseïs from me. I want to prove that I'm indispensable to the army. Please go to Zeus. He owes you. You released him from his shackles when the Olympians were trying to dethrone him. Tell him to assist the Trojans now that I've decided to absent myself from the battlefield. It's the only way to teach that bastard Agamemnon a lesson.'

I heaved a heavy sigh. I tried to argue him out of it but he was adamant. I plunged into the briny depths and swam across the Aegean in the direction of Mount Olympus. As soon as I had scaled its summit, I headed to Zeus' palace and grasped the father of gods and men by the knees in supplication.

'What's all this about, Thetis?' he inquired, lifting me up. 'It's not often you leave the watery deep and visit Olympus. It must be a matter of urgency.'

163

'It is indeed a matter of urgency, son of Cronus,' I replied. 'Achilles needs you to lend your support to the Trojans long enough for Agamemnon to realise that he can't win the war without him.'

Zeus' brow became furrowed. He squirmed awkwardly in his throne.

'This is a bad business,' he observed, shaking his silvery locks. 'It's going to infuriate Hera. You know how much she hates the Trojans. If she could have her way, she'd eat Priam raw, along with all his sons and daughters, and after that she'd devour all the Trojans as well. It all goes back to that rotten apple, which Eris [goddess of discord and contention] tossed among the guests at your wedding. Was it your decision or Peleus' to exclude Eris from the festivities?'

'Actually we both decided …'

'Well, it didn't do much good, did it? Eris invited herself along anyway. She always manages to get in on the act one way or another. The rotten apple – well, golden really – had the words "for the fairest" inscribed on it. As soon as all the goddesses saw it, each one thought it was meant for her and a screaming match broke out. If I hadn't intervened, they'd have scratched their eyes out.'

'Yes, but …'

'Eventually it was decided to hold a beauty contest to crown Miss Divine Goddess. The finalists were Aphrodite, Athena and my better half. There was a lot of talk about who should be the judge. None of the gods, goddesses, semi-gods, semi-goddesses, nymphs, naiads, satyrs, heroes and whatnot could be trusted to deliver an impartial verdict so, after much chuntering back and forth, we hit upon a nonentity, a shepherd boy named Paris, who used to graze his flocks on Mount Ida in Phrygia.'

'I know all this, Zeus. After all, it was my wedding that Eris spoiled.'

'The problem was that Paris couldn't decide between the three goddesses, however, so he asked them to strip naked for him. When he *still* couldn't make up his mind, each of them tried to bribe him. Athena offered him wisdom, Hera offered him success in war, and Aphrodite promised him the most beautiful woman in the world. He gave the apple to Aphrodite, as you know.'

'Yes …'

'It later transpired that Paris was actually the son of Priam and Hecuba, king and queen of Troy. They'd exposed him as an infant because Hecuba dreamed that she had given birth to a firebrand. A seer interpreted this to mean that her son would be the cause of Troy's ruin. The sensible thing would have been to kill the child, but they couldn't do that, they were his parents, so they exposed him on Mount Ida, where, lo and behold, he was found by some shepherds, who brought him up. Shortly after the divine beauty contest Paris competed in an athletic contest that Priam was hosting and won all the prizes, whereupon his parents realised he was their son. They were so overjoyed that they completely ignored the prophecy that had led them to expose him in the first place. And that's how things began to unfold. Are you paying attention to all this, Thetis?'

'I am indeed, most attentively, most mighty one, but I know all this. I was wondering if you could ...'

'Anyway, what Aphrodite *hadn't* revealed to Paris was that Helen, the most beautiful woman in the world, happened to be married to Menelaus, king of Sparta. Soon after Priam had acknowledged Paris as his son, he sent him to Sparta to pay respects to his old friend. Trojans and Greeks were on good terms back then, you see, and Menelaus and Priam were guest friends. Their ties of friendship went back generations, which makes this damned war they're now fighting all the more upsetting. Helen's abduction or theft – call it what you like – was the cause of the Trojan War. It was also the cause of Hera's violent hatred of Troy, because Paris, a Trojan, had insulted her, the queen of heaven no less. In short, I know this is going to end badly if I agree to your request. Do you see now why I'm so hesitant?'

'Yes, of course, I do, and I'm sorry to put you in this quandary, but you do owe me, father of gods and men, and I have to warn you that I won't be coming to your help ever again, if you don't honour your debt.'

'Very well,' Zeus replied, heaving a sigh from his mighty bosom.

'Do you swear a mighty oath?'

'I do.'

'Then bow your head. That'll make it official.'

Zeus inclined his head ever so slightly, whereupon an ominous roll of thunder ripped the air, causing the marble walls to shake, the gold-laced dining table to rattle, and the star-encrusted ceiling to wobble.

'I only hope Hera didn't hear that,' the father of gods and men said anxiously.

Hera

Of course I heard it. What do you think? A roll of thunder isn't something you can blithely ignore. I knew my husband was up to his old tricks, making a crooked deal behind my back. He doesn't deserve to be top god. He's a joke. And you can quote me on that. I'm the queen of heaven and the goddess of marriage. No matter how many affairs my husband has had, it's I who sit on the golden throne. I have eyes the size of an ox, which is why nothing escapes me.

I suspected something was up when I caught sight of Thetis threading her way down from Olympus to the sea. She had a shifty look about her. I grabbed hold of her and demanded she tell me what promise she had extracted from my husband. Imagine my fury when I learned that he'd agreed to favour the Trojans merely for the sake of honouring her son. What sense did that make? Thousands of Greeks would now have to perish just to satisfy the pride of one man. Because that's what it boils down to in the end. It's a simple matter of pride.

It's not just the deals Zeus concludes behind my back that infuriate me. It's his endless philandering. Charm on two legs. That's how he sees himself. The degradation I've had to put up with would have been bad enough if I were a mortal, let alone queen of heaven. He's even seduced a number of my priestesses, Io being a prime example.

Io served in my temple at Argos. When Zeus made his intentions clear to her, the girl reported him to her father, Inachus. Instead of praising his daughter for her decency, as he should have done, however, Inachus threw her out of his house. This pathetic specimen of manhood was more anxious about not offending Zeus than he was about safeguarding his daughter's honour.

I decided to nip my husband's desire in the bud by turning the girl into a white heifer. This only inflamed his desire all the more. Go figure.

So I sent all-seeing Argos – the creature with a hundred eyes – to watch over her. At least two of his eyes are always open. In response, Zeus dispatched Hermes from Olympus. Hermes put Argos to sleep with his wand and then smashed his head with a rock. Incidentally, that's why I'm associated with peacocks. I stuck Argos' hundred eyes on their tail feathers.

This made me even madder. I sent a gadfly to torment Io constantly. It had been hard enough already for Zeus to mate with her, given the fact that she was a heifer, but this made matters a lot worse since now she was always wriggling.

Io wandered all over the world, driven totally batty by the gadfly. She crossed from Europe into Asia by means of what we call today the Bosporus in her honour ('Bosporus' means 'Ox-crossing'). Eventually she arrived at the Caucasus Mountains, where she encountered the Titan Prometheus, chained to a rock. He was undergoing excruciating suffering because of Zeus, so they had a lot in common. Prometheus informed her that she would one day give birth to a child called Epaphus and that a descendant of his would overthrow Zeus, just as Zeus' father, Cronus, had overthrown *his* father, Uranus.

When the gong for dinner rang shortly after Thetis' departure, all the gods took their seats in the banqueting hall. I was determined to give Zeus a piece of my mind. I've never had any qualms about giving him a hard time in front of the other gods.

'You're always trying to deceive me,' I said contemptuously. 'Why don't you have the courage to confront me openly? How can you expect your brothers and sisters to obey you when you yourself behave in such an underhand way? Shame on you, Zeus!'

I know I got under his skin because he raised his fist as if about to strike me. Luckily for him, he thought better of it. If he'd followed through with it, there's no knowing what the consequences would have been.

Realising that an almighty row was about to break out, my son, Hephaestus, struggled to his feet and began replenishing our drinking cups. Owing to his clumsiness, however, most of the wine splashed onto the floor. Soon everyone was laughing uproariously. Even Zeus himself smiled.

I knew that the best way to get what I wanted and interrupt the Trojan assault was to arouse Zeus with uncontrollable desire. The problem was that he hadn't shown any interest in me sexually for aeons.

So I went to Aphrodite and got her to give me a sexy undergarment to wear. Next I went to Hypnos, god of sleep, and persuaded him to make Zeus fall asleep after our lovemaking.

Zeus was monitoring the war from Mount Ida on Crete. I told Sleep to hide in one of the pine trees. As soon as he saw me, his eyes almost literally popped out of their sockets.

'Hera!' he exclaimed, masking a giant erection beneath his loose-fitting gown. 'What a pleasant surprise. A *very* pleasant surprise. What are you doing here?'

'I'm on my way to the ends of the earth to visit Oceanus and Tethys,' I replied, assuming an air of innocence. 'I've heard their marriage is a bit rocky. I thought I'd see if I can be of any help.'

'What a good friend you are. Before you run off to the ends of the earth, however, why don't you lie down beside me for a while? You look ravishing. I'll be honest with you. I've never felt as much desire for any woman as I do for you right now, and I've felt quite a bit of desire for quite a few women in my time.'

The jerk then proceeded to rattle off the names of ten or more women he'd slept with, all of whom – he declared – I surpassed in beauty. What a plonker!

'That's quite a compliment,' I replied suavely. 'I feel very proud to be in such exalted company.'

'I'm being serious, Hera,' he went on. 'You look absolutely stunning. By the way, where did you get that sexy undergarment? I'm used to seeing you in that formless floral housecoat. Things are definitely looking up.'

'Do you like it?'

'Do I like it? Are you kidding? Come and lie down beside me.'

Zeus patted the plush sward and slapped me on the buttocks. I gritted my teeth. As soon as he had enfolded us in a cloud to give us privacy, he began humping me. As usual, it was all over in an instant. Then he was out for the count, snoring loudly.

With Zeus out of the picture, the Greeks returned to the offensive. The sea, acting under orders from Poseidon, surged forward just at the moment when Hector was about to set fire to the ships and drove the Trojans all the way back to the walls of their city. For a few brief glorious moments I took delight in seeing my Greeks on a killing spree.

As soon as Zeus woke up and realised what had happened, he was incandescent with rage.

'I'll make you pay dearly for this, Hera. Tartarus is too good for you,' he bawled.

Then he hurried back up to Olympus, cursing and spluttering. He doesn't scare me in the least. He knew I'd got the better of him.

Recently he and I had been arguing about whether men or women experience a more intense orgasm. In the end we decided to ask Teiresias to adjudicate. Teiresias had come across a pair of snakes in the foothills of Mount Cithaeron. When he saw they were mating, he struck them with his staff, whereupon, lo and behold, he turned into a woman. Seven years later he returned to the same spot and, as luck would have it, a pair of snakes was *again* mating. The spell was reversed and he turned back into a man. His mixed gender therefore made him eminently well-qualified to pronounce upon the intensity of orgasms.

'OK, Teiresias,' I said. 'Which is more pleasurable orgasm-wise, experiencing it as a man or as a woman?'

'As a woman by far,' he replied without a moment's hesitation. 'In fact it's ten times better as a woman. Wait. That's a slight exaggeration. I'd say it's nine times better.'

This was not something I wanted to become common knowledge. I was furious. I struck him blind on the spot. To compensate for his loss of sight, my husband granted him prophetic insight. So that's how he became the most famous seer of all time.

I hate the Trojans, as you know. They disrespected me. It's the Greeks I favour. Achilles, Agamemnon, Menelaus, Diomedes, Ajax the Bigger, Ajax the Smaller, Patroclus, Neoptolemus, Odysseus, Nestor: that lot. Nestor was the oldest Greek to fight at Troy. He'd already lived through three generations, so he was over sixty. He was known as silver-tongued because he always gave good advice. Well, not always, as you'll hear next. His son, Antilochus, also fought there.

Antilochus

Dad had tried to get Achilles to return to the battle before. When the Greeks began to panic under the Trojan advance he'd suggested sending an embassy to appeal to his better nature. Agamemnon, who now realised what a jerk he had been for insulting Achilles, readily agreed. He offered Achilles a bunch of stuff if he'd return to the battle. Dad suggested Odysseus, Phoenix and Ajax the Bigger should be the ones to make the appeal.

When the guys arrived, Achilles was playing the lyre, hanging out with Patroclus, his best buddy. He invited them to dinner. Odysseus was first to speak. He repeated word for word all the things that Agamemnon said he'd give Achilles in compensation. He said Agamemnon would return his girl Briseïs - he claimed he hadn't slept with her - and that Achilles could have his daughter as well. It didn't do any good. Achilles made a long speech about how it's pointless to work hard because you don't get any thanks for it and you die anyway. He ended by saying he was heading back home.

Then his old tutor, Phoenix, recounted the story of Meleager. Meleager was the son of Oeneus, king of the Aetolians. Oeneus had neglected to sacrifice to Artemis, so the goddess had sent a giant boar to ravage his territory. Meleager summoned hunters from all around, not only the Aetolians but also the Curetes, a local people, and eventually he killed the boar. Afterwards a violent quarrel broke out between the two peoples about how to divide up the spoils. So a war broke out between the Aetolians and the Curetes. Meleager fought on the Aetolian side and killed his mother's brother, one of the Curetes. His mother cursed him and he withdrew from the battle. He resisted all pleas to return. He only relented when the Curetes were about to burn down his house. He died fighting them off.

Phoenix's point was that Achilles should return to the battle before things got worse and he ended up like Meleager, fighting for nothing and dying anyway. Achilles was completely unmoved. It was only when Ajax said they were wasting their time and should leave him to it that Achilles undertook to rejoin the battle when the Trojans were at the point of burning their ships.

This then was the situation when Patroclus arrived at our tent. Achilles had heard things were going badly for us. Lots of our best men had suffered injury during Hector's onslaught. Diomedes had been shot in the foot, Odysseus had been wounded in his ribcage, our field doctor, Machaon, had been struck in the right shoulder, and Ajax the Bigger had been forced to retreat under a barrage of spear thrusts.

'Welcome, son of Menoetius,' Nestor said with his customary grace. 'Would you care for a beaker of wine?'

'I don't have time,' Patroclus replied. 'Achilles has sent me to find out how the war is going.'

'We can't hold out much longer. I've got an idea, though. What if Achilles agreed to lend you his armour? You could fight in his place. The Trojans would be intimidated and they might even lose heart. It's worth a chance, don't you think? Otherwise – I hate to say it – but I think our cause is lost.'

'That's a great idea, Nestor,' Patroclus said. 'I think he's beginning to feel some pity for the Greeks. I'll see what I can do.'

Patroclus exited our tent and was gone in a flash.

'Good luck!' I shouted.

He was in tears when he arrived back at Achilles' tent. It seems that the sight of so many wounded men had affected him deeply.

Achilles was lying on his bed when Patroclus returned. A slave was seated on a stool at its foot. He was trimming Achilles' toenails.

'What on earth's the matter with you, Patroclus?' Achilles asked scornfully. 'Why are you snivelling? Has mummy spanked you?'

'It's not funny, Achilles,' Patroclus replied. 'Our comrades are dropping like flies. Hector is about to set fire to our ships. Only a heartless brute would be unmoved by what I've just seen. If you still refuse to join the fray, at least lend me your armour. Then the Trojans will think you're back. With the aid of the gods, I might just be able to turn the course of the battle. But there isn't a second to lose.'

'I never intended my anger to last forever,' Achilles said, rising from his bed and dismissing the slave. 'I promised I would return to the fight once Hector set fire to the ships. By all means borrow my armour. That way you will win me honour. Just one word of warning, though. Don't try scaling the walls. Merely drive the Trojans back from our ships. It is not fated for you to take the city. That's my destiny and mine alone. Is that clear?'

'As clear as mud,' Patroclus replied with a smile.

He slipped Achilles' breastplate over his head and began fastening the leather straps at the sides. Then he attached the greaves to his shins. Achilles prayed solemnly to Zeus: 'O Zeus, son of Cronus, father of gods and men, see no harm befalls my dear friend Patroclus.'

Much good *that* did.

'You look quite the hero,' Achilles said, giving Patroclus a hug just before he ascended his chariot. 'By which I mean you look just like me.'

Well, a lot happens in the heat of the battle. People get carried away and they don't think straight. They have to make decisions on the spur of the moment. To cut a long story short, Patroclus forgot all about Achilles' warning. Once he had driven the Trojans back to their city, he couldn't stop himself. He just had to scale the walls. He tried three times but on each occasion Apollo shoved him back, swatting him like a fly with the back of his hand. When he tried a fourth time, the god lost all patience.

He found Hector, revealed Patroclus' identity to him, and urged him to engage in single combat. Once Patroclus' bluff had been called, it was as if the wind had been knocked out of his sails. He put up a valiant fight, but he was no match for Hector.

I was standing a few yards away when Hector struck him in the belly with his spear. The blow was so forceful that the tip of his spear came out the other side of his body. Patroclus fell to the ground, his armour crashing.

I ran to Achilles with the news.

'Son of Peleus,' I gasped breathlessly. 'Patroclus has fallen. The Greeks and the Trojans are fighting over his naked body. Hector of the shining helmet has seized your armour.'

I don't want to be too harsh on Achilles. Speak well of the dead is my motto. And besides, he has suffered enough. Not a day passed when he didn't ask himself how he could have let this happen. Not just let this happen, but *cause* it to happen. He had seen himself as a man of principle, one who defiantly opposed an authoritarian scoundrel. And he threw away the lives of countless others by nursing his precious dignity.

Achilles

Yes, blame me all you want. I deserve it.

The moment I learned that Patroclus had died, it was as if everything I loved and everything I believed in had been destroyed. I couldn't return to the fighting because I didn't have any armour, so I did the only thing I could do. I roared in anger. I roared three times. I roared so loudly that twelve Trojans died. This enabled the Greeks to retrieve Patroclus' body. Then I gave myself up to grief. I even beheaded twelve Trojan prisoners in an effort to appease his spirit. I wasn't in my right mind. I acknowledge that.

My mother asked Hephaestus to make me a new suit of armour. I'd never seen her so upset. She knew my death was close at hand. For days on end I couldn't bring myself to bury Patroclus, so the gods poured nectar and ambrosia into his nostrils to keep his body fresh.

I called an assembly. I told Agamemnon that we needed to move on. He made a long-winded apology. Well, not an apology at all really. He blamed Zeus for befuddling his wits; not just Zeus, but also Fate and the Furies, and what he called Delusion. He blamed everyone and everything. Then he offered me reparations: tripods, cauldrons, horses, and lots more besides. Finally he handed Briseïs back to me. I was still heartbroken. I could think only of Patroclus.

When Briseïs saw Patroclus' body, she burst into floods of tears. 'Beloved Patroclus, you were such a good friend to me,' she cried. 'You comforted me when I was mourning the death of my husband, whom Achilles had killed. And then, when Achilles and I began to develop feelings for each other, you said you would persuade him to marry me. I will sorely miss you.'

Once I got my new suit of golden armour, I didn't hold back. I began killing Trojans indiscriminately. I killed so many that the River Xanthus couldn't swallow all the corpses I tossed into its jaws.

I only wanted to fight Hector, however. I caught up with him outside the city gates. He took one look at me and fled. I chased him three times around the walls. Eventually he stopped running and turned around to face me. He knew the game was up.

'Let's agree that whoever wins the contest will respect his opponent's corpse,' Hector pleaded.

'No way. It would be against the natural order. I hate you with every fibre of my being.'

We took up our positions and brandished our spears. Hector threw his first. It struck the boss of my shield without penetrating it. Then I threw mine. It shaved his neck, causing a jet of blood to spurt out. He fell to the ground.

'Please don't desecrate my corpse,' he begged, as I towered over him. 'I don't want to end up as a feast for the beasts and birds!'

'No more pleading, you wretched scoundrel. I wish I had the strength to hack the flesh from your bones piece by piece and eat you raw for all the things you've made me suffer.'

I pulled my spear from his body and stripped off his armour. He was wearing the suit of armour I had lent Patroclus.

Soon the Greeks collected around his body. They jeered at him, jabbing his body with the tips of their spears.

'He's much softer now than he was a moment ago,' one joked.

I attached Hector's body to my chariot so that his head dragged in the dust and then I circled around Troy under the horrified gaze of his wife and his parents, who observed the gruesome scene from the ramparts.

Priam

Achilles has slain so many of my sons. I didn't care half as much for the whole damned pack of them as I did for Hector. Hector was my pride and joy.

For twelve days Achilles had his horses drag Hector's corpse around the mound where his friend, Patroclus, was laid out. In the end, even the gods were sickened and forced him to desist.

That same day I received a visit from Iris, Zeus' messenger. I was lying in the dirt, my head covered in dung. As soon as I saw her standing before me, I knelt and bowed my head.

'I've been sent here by Zeus,' she explained. 'He tells you to go to Achilles and ask for Hector's body. He won't kill you. There's nothing to fear.'

With that she departed. I didn't waste a second. I ordered my sons to prepare a cart and tether two mules to it. Then I filled the cart with baskets of treasures from the storeroom. When my wife saw what I was doing, she began screaming.

'Are you out of your wits, you stupid old man? Do you think Achilles will take pity on you when he sees you? I'd set my teeth in his liver if I could. Your place is beside me. We should be consoling each other with memories of our son at this moment.'

'I've made my mind up, Hecuba. Don't try to change it. I can't leave our son's body to rot.'

I summoned my groom and we set off. I followed behind the cart on horseback. When it began to get dark, we halted to water the mules in the river that runs past the tomb of Ilus, the founder of Ilium. Just as we were about to set off again, a youth approached us. We were both seized with green fear, a particularly nasty variety. When he got close, however, he smiled and took my hand gently.

'Are you Trojans?' he inquired. 'What are you doing here at this time of night? Have you lost your way? Don't worry. I'll see that no harm comes to you. I serve under Achilles.'

'Some god must be protecting us to put you in our path,' I replied. 'I'm King Priam. I'm actually on my way to see your commander. Can you give me any news of my son's body?'

'There's nothing to worry about,' the youth replied. 'The gods have preserved it intact. It's as fresh as it was the moment the breath left his body.'

I tried to offer him one of the gifts I had brought with me, but he gently pushed me away.

'I don't want anything,' he said. 'Just follow me. I'll escort you to my commander's tent in safety.'

He was as good as his word. When we came within sight of the guards, my heart again took fright. Instantly our divine guide whipped out his magic wand.

'Achilles' tent is that one over there,' he said, pointing. 'Go in peace and success attend your mission.'

'God of merchants and travellers …' I began. But before I could say another word, his winged sandals were bearing him aloft.

I drew back the flap and entered Achilles' tent. He was almost struck dumb when he saw me. I fell at his knees, grasped his hands in mine and gently kissed them: the hands that had slaughtered so many of my sons.

'Please don't be angry with me coming here like this unannounced,' I begged. 'Think of me as your father. I'm sure he loves to hear word of your exploits. I'm a father too. So many of my sons are dead because of the war. I'm here to offer you gifts in return for the body of Hector. I'm more pitiful than any man alive. I've just kissed the hands of the man who has killed my sons. Who would do such a thing?'

I had no idea what he would do. I was half expecting him to slit my throat. Instead he lifted me gently to my feet. Then we both began weeping. After a few moments he pushed me away and dried his tears.

'You must have nerves of iron to come here, Priam,' he said. 'No one else would dare to do what you have just done. Here, take a seat beside me. I recognise your pain. Life is full of misery. Zeus has two urns placed on the doorsill of his palace on Olympus. In one urn is good fortune, in the other bad fortune. If you're lucky he gives you good fortune mixed with bad. If you're not, you just get bad fortune. No one gets only good fortune.'

'That sums life up pretty well,' I agreed. 'I'm impatient to see my son's body. Would you kindly allow that please?'

'I'd already decided to return the body,' Achilles replied.

He summoned his slaves, ordered them to wash Hector's body and then covered it with a shroud. When they had finished, he tenderly lifted it up and laid it in my cart.

'Forgive me, Patroclus,' he said. 'Priam has given me a generous ransom in return for yielding up Hector's corpse. I'll make sure that a large portion of it is placed on your grave.'

'I have one more request,' I said tentatively.

'Name it.'

'Can we make a truce so that I can perform a proper funeral for Hector.'

'How long do you need?'

'Twelve days. Ten days to mourn, one day to hold a feast in his honour, and one to conduct the cremation.'

'Agreed. But now you need to rest. I'll get you a blanket.'

I lay down and fell asleep immediately. Shortly after midnight I felt a tap on my shoulder. I woke up to find myself staring into the face of my divine conductor, Hermes.

'Are you out of your mind?' he demanded. 'You need to get going immediately. If Agamemnon finds you're here, he won't show you any mercy. He'll demand a huge ransom.'

I sprung to my feet and roused my driver. Silently we made our way through the sleeping ranks of the Greeks. By the time we got within sight of Troy, the sun was rising. I saw my daughter Cassandra standing atop the citadel.

Cassandra

I'd been up all night. I couldn't sleep a wink.

As soon as I saw the dust from the mule cart rising in the early morning haze, I shouted out, 'Trojans, come and look at Hector, our pride and joy, returning home!'

Seconds later the gates of the city were flung open and the entire citizenry exited. Hector's wife, Andromache, was in the lead.

'Think of our son, Astyanax,' she used to say to her husband. 'Imagine what his life will be like if anything happens to you. Nothing is worse than being an orphan. Just picture him going from table to table, begging. One man will give him a crust of bread, but another will hit him and order him away. Is that the future you want for him?'

Neoptolemus about to kill Priam over the body of his dead grandson Astyanax.

Hector never listened. He knew he had to fight. He couldn't have lived with himself otherwise. That was the kind of person he was.

I know better than Andromache, however. I know the fate that is awaiting Astyanax and it's far worse than the one she imagined. Achilles' son, Neoptolemus, is going to toss him from the walls of our city. The Greeks won't want him growing up to avenge his father, so they're not going to leave any messy loose ends behind. This is my terrible destiny: to see the future sufferings of my loved ones and be powerless to avert them.

An irreversible chain reaction has been set in motion. Less than a year from now Troy will be a smoking ruin. And it's all because of Aphrodite.

Aphrodite

I'm always being blamed for human misery. I'm the goddess of love and beauty. That's right, love. What's wrong with love? It's just that mortals have a knack for making bad choices and screwing up. Gods do as well, of course. Let's not forget that.

To be honest, I'm pretty screwed up too. Why in gods' names did I marry Hephaestus? I'm drop-dead gorgeous, whereas my husband is a misshapen idiot. Can you blame me for having an affair with the nimble-footed god of war?

Matters came to a head when Hephaestus said, 'I'm off to Lemnos today. I'm visiting the Sintians whose speech is strange. Don't bother to wait up.'

'Safe travels,' I replied, blowing him a kiss.

As soon as he was out the door, I put on some lipstick, slipped on something to grace my sinuous body, checked myself out in a bronze mirror, and skipped off with dainty footsteps to find my lover.

Ares was lounging indolently on a couch when I burst into his palace.

'We've got a whole day for some rough and tumble,' I said excitedly.

'Your palace or mine?' Ares asked, springing to his feet with his customary alacrity.

'Mine. My bed is so much more comfortable than yours. After all, it was made by a master craftsman.'

We both giggled. Then we ran hand in hand to my palace. Ares thrust me down on the bed and tore off dress, exposing my luscious swelling breasts and creamy thighs. His divine member slipped easily inside me and we went at it hammer and tongs. Ares was just about to climax when a net suddenly dropped down on us. It was made of very fine cables, invisible to the naked eye. It locked us in a tighter embrace than I had ever experienced from the arms of either a man or a god.

No matter how much we wriggled, we couldn't free ourselves. All we could do was lie there like a pair of trussed turkeys. I felt Ares grow limp.

Hephaestus suddenly emerged from under the bed, where he had been hiding.

He hobbled over to the window and shouted at the top of his voice. 'Zeus and all you gods! Look how my sluttish wife is disrespecting me with destructive Ares, all because of my deformity. I wish I'd never been born.'

Within seconds the gods had arrived, all eager to know what the fuss was about. The goddesses, to their credit, stayed away.

'Ares has got his comeuppance,' one of the gods quipped. 'Hephaestus isn't such a slouch after all.'

Apollo turned to Hermes and said, 'How would you like to be lying in bed with Aphrodite, tied in mighty chains?'

'I'd happily submit to being tied in chains three times as tight just to be having it off with lovely Aphrodite,' Hermes replied, smirking. 'And I wouldn't care if the goddesses were looking on. In fact it would be a plus!'

At this all the gods laughed uproariously. What a prat my husband is. He had been cheated on and had only made things worse by publicising his humiliation.

My favourite lover was Adonis. How to describe him? Adonis was, well, an Adonis. We had great sex together. The trouble was he was a daredevil. He liked to live on the edge, owing to the fact that his brain was pumped full of dopamine. His favourite sport was hunting. I was always telling him to be careful, but he laughed in my face. One day he was gored in the thigh by a boar. He bled to death in my arms. It was from his blood that the flower known as anemone came into being. It's a perpetual reminder of his beauty.

Adonis was the product of an incestuous relationship between a father and a daughter. It was his daughter, Myrrha, who had initiated the relationship by seducing him without his knowing that she was his daughter. When her father found out, he was ready to kill her. Myrrha prayed for me to save her and because I sympathise with love no matter what form it takes I turned her into a myrrh tree.

My older son is Priapus. Priapus walks around all day long with a giant erection (hence the word 'priapism', which denotes that condition).

The picture of someone with a giant erection might sound rather comical, but it's actually extremely painful because he can't do anything to relieve it. Whenever he sees a comely nymph, for instance, his penis immediately becomes flaccid. This is all due to the fact that Hera cursed Priapus for my beating her in the beauty contest. The first time he couldn't get it up was when he was about to rape Hestia, goddess of the hearth. Just as he was on the point of entry, he heard an ass bray and that took the wind entirely out of his sails. And now it happens all the time. He's only erect when there's no one around to give him an erection.

My younger son is Cupid, whose father is Ares. He's warlike, just like his father. He loves to play with his bow and arrow. He pretends to be innocent, but he can be very beguiling. Whenever I want someone to fall in love, he shoots one of his gold-tipped arrows into their heart. He did that to Phaedra, who fell in love with her stepson. If I want someone to reject another person's advances, he uses an iron-tipped arrow.

Nobody mocks the little fellow without paying heavily for it. After Apollo had slain the python that was plaguing the inhabitants of Delphi, he went around bragging about how great he was. It was just his bad luck to encounter Cupid. Apollo told him contemptuously that his antics with a bow and arrow were child's play.

'What's so special about getting men and women to fall in love?' Apollo demanded. 'It takes real guts to kill a python. Something you'll never have. You're just a namby-pamby.'

Not long afterwards Apollo got the hots for a naiad named Daphne. The instant his eyes locked onto her, Cupid shot a gold-tipped arrow into his heart, driving him wild with passion. Then he shot an iron-tipped arrow into Daphne's heart, causing her to loathe the god with equal passion.

'My darling, I've never seen anyone more beautiful,' Apollo expostulated in a plaintive tone that would have turned a human stomach, let alone that of a naiad. 'You're a radiant, dazzling beauty. I'm the god Apollo.'

Well, if this little speech was supposed to impress her, it fell lamentably short. Even without the effect of Cupid's iron-tipped arrow in her breast, Daphne would have realised that Apollo only wanted one thing and that once he had got it, he'd be on his merry way.

'Keep your hands away from me, you dirty beast!' Daphne screamed, screwing her face up in disgust. 'I don't want anything to do with you. I wouldn't have sex with you if you were the last god alive! As for claiming you love me, we both know you're only after one thing.'

Apollo pursuing Daphne.

Daphne ran off and Apollo followed in hot pursuit, his ardour inflamed by her rejection of him. Eventually she reached the bank of a river fringed by a line of laurel trees. Apollo thundered up behind her. She could feel his hot breath on her skin. When he was within two bows' length of her, she called upon the river by name.

183

'Save me, Father Peneus!' she implored.

Apollo was on the point of grabbing her hair when the river answered her prayer. Her fingertips began to sprout leaves, while her trunk – I mean her human trunk – became a tree trunk, resembling one of the laurel trees on the bank. Apollo tried to kiss her but the tree's bark closed around her lips. Daphne, or the girl he had loved, was no more.

Hero and Leander.

Human love almost always ends badly. Take the story of Hero and Leander, the archetypal long-distance lovers. Hero lived on the north side of the Hellespont, whereas Leander inconveniently lived on the south side. I never understood why they didn't move in together.

Every evening Leander swam across the Hellespont, guided by a lamp that Hero set in a tower. Every evening she waited for him on the beach, eager to catch sight of his arms carving the crinkled water. One evening Leander set out in a storm. A howling wind blew Hero's lamp out, Leander lost his way and drowned in the heaving waters. When Hero discovered his dead body on the shore the next day, she threw herself off the tower.

The love of Pyramus and Thisbe also ran aground. Distance didn't separate this pair. On the contrary, they lived next door to one another. Their parents objected to their affair, so the only way they could communicate was through a chink in the party wall between the two houses.

'This sucks,' Pyramus said one day in his direct way through the chink. 'Let's meet outside the city at Ninus' tomb and have some fun.'

They agreed to meet the next day. Thisbe arrived first, only to discover a lioness fresh from a recent kill licking its bloody chops.

'Save me, Heavenly Twins!' she cried as she fled, leaving behind her veil.

Two minutes later Pyramus arrived. Finding Thisbe's veil covered in blood, he assumed she was dead. Heartbroken, he drew his dagger from his belt and thrust it deep into his belly. As if things couldn't get any worse, Thisbe returned a minute later to find him expiring. Heartbroken in turn, she extracted the dagger from Pyramus' belly and plunged it deep into her heart.

The only happy love story I know of involves a sculptor named Pygmalion, who had a desire to create an ideal woman. As he chipped away at his statue of her, he became more and more enamoured of it. When he stood back to admire his finished creation, he couldn't refrain from embracing it.

He was so love-struck with Galatea, as he called the statue, that he asked me to make it come alive. I consented. When he touched her arm a moment later, it felt warm to his touch. A rosy glow began to spread to her cheeks and the next thing he knew her breasts were heaving.

Pygmalion about to fall in love with his statue of the incomparably beautiful Galatea.

Then there's the tragic story of my son, Aeneas and Queen Dido. When Troy fell, Aeneas escaped with his son, Ascanius, whom he held tightly by the hand. He carried his father Anchises on his back. His wife, Creusa, got somehow lost in the shuffle. He and a few Trojan refugees got on board ship headed west, hoping to found a new home. A few days after they set sail, however, a severe tempest forced Aeneas to dock at Carthage in Tunisia.

Carthage's queen, Dido, had been recently widowed and forced to flee from an unwelcome suitor. Her city was still under construction. It seemed like the perfect set up. Aeneas, too, was recently widowed and now homeless.

When Dido and Aeneas were out hunting one day, a storm broke out. They took refuge in a cave, where one thing quickly led to another. Shortly afterwards, however, Zeus sent his messenger Hermes down to remind Aeneas that he was on a mission to found Rome.

'I hadn't forgotten,' Aeneas said. 'Tell Zeus I just need a few days to sort things out here.'

'You're to leave tomorrow,' Hermes replied curtly, flying off into the stratosphere.

'I had a visit from Hermes today,' Aeneas told Dido later as they were lying in bed. 'I'm afraid I have to leave.'

Dido sat up in bed.

'What did you say?'

'I said I had a visit from Hermes. He told me Zeus has ordered me to leave.'

'Zeus? Did you say Zeus?' Dido exclaimed disdainfully. 'What's Zeus got to do with this? Are you really so important to him? What a pathetic excuse. Couldn't you come up with something better? You're a cad and I hope you rot in Hades.'

Aeneas sailed off at dawn the next day. When Dido saw his ships disappearing over the horizon, she cursed him and his descendants in perpetuity. Then she ordered her slaves to build a pyre. She told her sister, Anna, that she was going to burn Aeneas' personal belongings. Instead she climbed on top of the pyre and fell upon Aeneas' sword.

Eventually Aeneas reached the coast of Italy, known as Hesperia, the Western Land, where he married Lavinia, the daughter of the local king, Latinus. His son, Ascanius, founded a city called Alba Longa and a descendant of his, called Romulus, founded Rome. So I'm the mother of the Roman race.

I also happen to be very jealous. The girl I was most jealous of was Psyche. She was so beautiful that bread-eaters began worshipping her instead of me.

Psyche

It's not my fault if I'm drop dead gorgeous. I have golden ringlets, pearly white teeth, breasts like ripe melons, skin the colour of ivory, a tinkling laugh, and hips that rotate wildly. You name it. I've got it. It's not been an easy life. Men couldn't handle me. My beauty intimidated them. What a bunch of wimps.

'I've got to find a husband for you, Psyche,' my father said one day. 'I can't support you and your sisters forever. I'm going to consult the Delphic Oracle and see what Apollo has to say.'

I went to my bedroom to have a little weep. I felt so lonely. Would Mr Right never come along?

My father returned a few days later and called me into his study.

'Well?' I asked anxiously. 'What did Apollo say?'

'The good news is that you're going to be married at once,' he replied, avoiding my eye. 'I'll buy you a wedding gown.'

'And the bad news?' I asked, sensing his unease.

'You're to walk to the top of the nearest hill dressed in a wedding gown and marry a serpent.'

'Marry a serpent? No way!' I responded angrily.

'I'm just telling you what the oracle said. Don't blame me,' my father replied tetchily.

For several days I remained locked in my room, refusing my father's appeals to come out. I have a tenacious grasp on life, however, so eventually I decided there was nothing for it but to go along with Apollo's recommendation.

'I'm sure it won't be as bad as it sounds,' my father said feebly, kissing me goodbye.

I felt a bit of a prat walking through the town in a wedding gown and holding a bouquet. Kids jeered at me. When I reached the hill,

I discarded my bouquet, hitched my dress up to my knees, and began climbing. It was blisteringly hot and soon I was sweating all over.

When I eventually reached the summit, there wasn't a single serpent to be seen anywhere. I even peered under every rock, but without any luck. It was getting dark, so I lay down on a bed of leaves. I fell asleep immediately.

When I awoke the next morning, I found myself stretched out on a manicured lawn fringed by palm trees rising twelve feet in the air. At the far end of the lawn was a sumptuous palace with marble walls and a gold roof. I got up, dusted my wedding dress down, and walked towards it. The grass felt spongy under my feet. The porch was smothered in geraniums and a bougainvillea tree stood on either side of the door. I was about to knock when I discovered it was ajar, so I pushed it open and entered. The interior was cavernous. Embroidered tapestries hung from the walls.

After wandering through room after room, I eventually found myself inside a large banqueting hall. In the centre was a long table made out of gleaming ebony, with velvet upholstered chairs down both sides. A magnificent repast had been laid out, including my all-time favourite, fruit pig haggis with oat crumbs and apple chutney. I sat down at the head of the table and began to tuck in. The food was heavenly and I gorged myself on it. When I'd finished, I washed it down with a large goblet of fizzy pink wine, which I drained in a single draught.

Having satisfied my hunger and thirst, I continued my exploration. As the light began to fade I found myself in a room with dark velvet drapes. Tall candles in sconces cast flickering shadows on the ceiling. A large bed lay in the centre. I untied the straps of my dress, let it fall to the ground, stepped out of it, and plonked myself down on the bed, spread-eagled. Before I knew what had hit me, I was fast asleep.

Suddenly I woke with a jolt. I had the realisation that I wasn't alone. Seconds later I felt a hand gently exploring the contours of my body. It was an entirely new sensation and curiously pleasurable. Though I couldn't see my companion, I guessed right away that he must be a god. I debated whether to resist him, but in the end, what the heck, I thought, and let nature takes its course.

When I awoke next morning, the sun was flooding the room and birds were chirping on the windowsill. I felt around the bed for my mysterious lover but he was nowhere to be found.

Psyche and Cupid.

This delightful routine lasted for weeks. By day I wandered through the palace marvelling at its delights and then, when the light began to fade, I returned to the velvet-draped bedroom to await my inexhaustible lover.

Like most men I've known, he wasn't much of a talker. One night, however, as we were lying in bed after a particularly energetic bout of lovemaking, he idly mentioned that my sisters had been inquiring about me.

I immediately sat up.

'Cressida and Hermione have been asking about me? I was thinking about them only today. Let's invite them to the palace.'

'I don't think that would be a good idea,' my lover replied.

'Why on earth not?'

'There's something that I haven't told you yet, Psyche.'

'Yes, it's about time you revealed your name.'

'I don't mean that. What I have to tell you is that you're pregnant.'

'I'm pregnant? How come you were keeping that from me as well?'

'I thought you might have guessed. Most girls do.'

'Well, I'm not most girls, in case you hadn't noticed,' I commented with a touch of pique.

'Anyway, that's beside the point. Your sisters will want to persuade you to discover my identity and that would definitely *not* be a good thing.'

'Why? What's so special about you? And why is it beside the point, as you put it? It may be beside *your* point but it certainly isn't beside *my* point.'

'I can't answer any of those questions right now, Psyche. You'll just have to trust me.'

'Trust you! That's what all cads and bounders say. You've got me pregnant and I don't even know your name. If you don't allow me to invite my sisters, I'm leaving right now. I want them to see how I live. They'll turn green with envy.'

I leapt out of bed and started to put on my dress. I was furious.

'OK,' he said. 'Have it your own way. But just be careful. Remember what I said.'

A week later my sisters arrived at the palace. As soon as I opened the door to reveal the magnificence of the interior, their breath was completely taken away.

'I think I'm going to have to sit down,' said Cressida. 'I feel quite faint.'

'Well, I never,' remarked Hermione. 'Who's the lucky man?'

'I don't actually know,' I replied offhandedly. 'I'm certain he's a god, though.'

'You don't actually know who he is?' Cressida repeated, looking at her sister in stunned disbelief. 'And you've let this god, as you call him, take advantage of you? Are you a simpleton? At least give us a description of him.'

'I can't. I've never seen him.'

My two sisters both stared at me wide-eyed.

'What do you mean you've never seen him?' Hermione asked.

'He arrives in the night and leaves before dawn,' I explained, beginning to feel just a tad foolish.

Cressida started tut-tutting furiously. 'There's only one explanation I can think of for him not wanting to reveal himself to you.'

'What's that?' I asked.

'Isn't it obvious? He's no more a god than I am. He's a perfect monster.'

'A monster!' I cried in alarm, thinking of Apollo's prophecy about having to marry a snake. 'Maybe he's just a bit shy. That's not a bad quality in a man.'

My sisters snorted derisively.

'You can take it from us that he's a certified monster, Psyche,' Hermione said. 'You always were simple-minded. You've got yourself into a right pickle. Anyway, there's only one way to find out. You're going to have to sneak a look at him while he's asleep. If he's not a monster, what's he got to hide?'

Reluctantly I agreed. That night, before going to bed to await the arrival of my mystery man, I hid an oil lamp under the bed. We made love as usual and after he had climaxed six times within half an hour he fell asleep. I lifted the lamp, lit it and directed it towards his face. For good measure I'd also hidden a knife under the bed. I was ready to slash his neck if it turned out he really *was* a monster.

Instead I found myself gazing into the face of the most handsome youth I had ever seen. I leant forward and kissed him lightly on the lips. In so doing, I tilted the lamp, causing the flame to scorch his shoulder. Instantly he sprang out of bed and began fluttering his wings. Then he shot out the window like a caged bird sensing freedom and soared aloft. I leapt out of bed and just managed to grab hold of one of his legs. For a few moments I was borne upwards, but my strength soon gave way and I fell to earth, landing without injury on the plush, manicured lawn.

I was heartbroken. For months I wandered up and down the earth, searching for him everywhere. One day I came to a sanctuary of Aphrodite. I entered the temple and abased myself before a statue of the goddess.

'Dear laughter-loving goddess,' I prayed. 'My heart is broken. Please help me find my lover. I will die otherwise.'

Suddenly the statue came to life and I found myself staring into the eyes of Aphrodite herself. I was nearly blinded by the radiance that was emanating from her.

'What is love if you don't have any trust?' the goddess demanded scornfully. 'You don't deserve my help. You're not a true lover. You're a faithless fraud.'

'I acknowledge my error, mistress,' I replied, bursting into tears at her stern rebuke. 'I should never have questioned his judgement. I just want to see him one more time to ask for his forgiveness.'

'I will grant your wish on condition that you perform one task for me,' she declared.

'I'll do anything,' I said earnestly.

'You see this heap of seeds?' she said, pointing to a mound the size of a house stacked in a corner of the temple. 'It's got lots of different varieties. I want you to sort them out into separate piles. I'll give you one night to complete the task. What are you waiting for? The clock's ticking. Good luck.'

I knew it was an impossible task. As soon as she departed, however, an army of ants crawled out from under the floor and began lifting the seeds onto their backs. When Aphrodite returned at dawn next day hoping to witness my frustration, she found twelve neat piles laid out on the flagstones of the temple floor.

'How on earth did you manage it?' she demanded, dumbfounded.

'I had some help,' I confessed.

'That doesn't count then,' she said angrily. 'That's cheating. You'll have to perform another task for me.'

She took me outside the temple and pointed to a river in full spate in the valley below.

'You see that golden fleece over there? The one that's hanging from a tree on the far bank? I want you to fetch it for me. I hope you know how to swim.'

'I don't,' I said in despair.

'That's too bad. Don't expect me to attend your funeral.'

Tentatively I descended to the river bank. The water was far too deep for me to wade across. Besides, there were jagged rocks and I would have cut myself to pieces. I sat down and began to howl my eyes out.

'Cheer up, Psyche,' whispered some reeds that were growing by the bank. 'If you look closely you'll see that there are bits of the golden fleece attached to the briars that are growing on this side. Just gather those up.'

'Thanks, reeds!' I said gratefully, leaping to my feet.

Minutes later I returned to the sanctuary with an armload of shiny, sparkling scraps of gold fleece.

Aphrodite was astonished yet again. 'How did you manage *that*?'

'This time I had some advice,' I explained.

'Well, that doesn't count either,' she replied, even more enraged. 'Here, take this bucket. Go to the River Styx and fill it with water. Watch out for corpses. I'm sure they'll be reluctant to let a pretty girl like you return to earth.'

I picked up the bucket and began walking in the direction of Hades. Eventually I came to a cliff on the outskirts of the infernal region.

I tiptoed to the edge and gazed down at the River Styx. It was hundreds of feet below. I was about to dive in when an eagle flew past. It grabbed my bucket, swooped down to the river, and returned with it filled to the brim with water as black as pitch.

'Thanks, eagle!' I cried, as it disappeared upwards into the firmament.

I walked back to the sanctuary, labouring under the weight of the water.

Aphrodite didn't even bother to ask me what had happened this time.

'OK, this is the ultimate task. Enter Hades and bring me back a fragment of Persephone's beauty.'

'How on earth can I bring back a fragment of anyone's beauty?' I demanded. 'Beauty is an abstraction. It doesn't have parts. You should know.'

'I've given you your task,' Aphrodite replied. 'If you carry it out, I promise I won't stand in your way anymore. Otherwise you can forget about your lover forever.'

She was sure she had stumped me this time. To her utter surprise, however, I was back moments later. Or rather a vague outline of my body was back.

'I can hardly see you,' she said. 'You've been vaporised.'

'Yes, I know,' I replied. 'I was about to throw myself off a high tower in despair when the tower told me to take some food to charm Cerberus and an obol to pay Charon, plus a box to put the fragment in. It also warned me not to look at the fragment because if I did I would be enveloped in darkness. But you know what happens when you're told not to do something. You have to do it, right? Overcome with curiosity, I opened the box and peered at the fragment. That's why you can hardly see me. I'm enveloped in darkness, like the tower warned.'

'Tut-tut,' said laughter-loving Aphrodite with a laugh. 'That serves you right for being curious. You're just like Pandora. Now you'll have to stay invisible forever.'

With that she left. What she didn't know was that my lover Cupid had been assisting me throughout. He now sped down to earth on his gold wings, landed beside me, and crammed the darkness back into the box.

'I had my suspicions you were helping me all along,' I said, throwing my arms around his wings and planting a moist kiss on his lips.

We soared back up to Mount Olympus, where Zeus granted me immortality. I got a round of applause from the Olympians, who,

Charon, ferryman of the dead.

when all is said and done, are quite a sentimental lot. Even my new mother-in-law put a brave face on it. I'm happy to say we have lived happily ever after. Not words you hear often in this line of business.

Talking about the phrase 'happily ever after', what was it like for Menelaus and Helen once they got back together? I've always wondered.

Helen

I know you've been aching to ask that question. Let's just say we made peace. Menelaus was sensible enough not to ask me too many questions and I was prudent enough not to venture too much information. The Trojan War was never about love. It was all about ownership, and pride.

Neither I nor my sister, Clytemnestra, were what you would call shining examples of wifely devotion, but I put that down to the men we've had the misfortune to marry.

Of course I'm partly to blame for the war. I'm not denying that. 'The face that launched a thousand ships.' That's how I'll be remembered. Well, I had to spread it around. Generosity is my middle name. And I've always liked men. But how could I ever have suspected that one little act of infidelity would have had such catastrophic, indeed genocidal, consequences?

I'm not a bad person. If you want bad, think of the Danaïds, the fifty daughters of Danaüs. They were contracted to marry the fifty sons of Aegyptus. Their father hated his twin brother, Aegyptus, with a passion, so he instructed his daughters to murder their bridegrooms on their wedding night. Forty-nine of them didn't think twice. They went ahead and butchered them. It was a bloodbath. Just like my sister Clytemnestra butchering Agamemnon. Only one – her name was Hypermnestra – didn't follow through.

'Hello, Lynceus,' Hypermnestra said to her bridegroom, when she went around to his house just as her sisters were sharpening their knives.

'Hello, Hypermnestra,' he replied. 'This is an unexpected pleasure. I thought we weren't supposed to see each other before our wedding.'

'I've decided to spare your life.'

'What did you say?' Lynceus demanded, jumping out of his chair. 'Why would you murder me?'

'Never mind that now. There's one condition, however.'

'OK, name it.'

'That we never have sex.'

'Never have sex? Why?'

'I prefer to remain a virgin all my life if you have no objections. Or if you do have objections, you'll know what to expect.'

'Fair enough,' Lynceus replied, as the piercing screams of the dying bridegrooms rang in his ears.

Lynceus and Hypermnestra lived happily ever after. Sex isn't always what it's cracked up to be, that's for sure.

The Danaïds, despite their unprepossessing track record, all found alternative husbands in due course. When they descended to Hades, however, they were condemned to carry water in leaky jars endlessly.

Back to me. I didn't have any choice in the matter. I was set up by Aphrodite. She'd told Paris he could have the most beautiful woman in the world if he awarded her first prize in the beauty contest. She never consulted me. I was just a pawn.

I rejected Paris many times when he wanted to have sex with me, but Aphrodite always forced me to submit to his demands.

'Take care I don't turn against you,' she said menacingly, 'Right now I love you, but I'm quite capable of hating you.'

The only Trojan who didn't give me the cold shoulder was Hector. Hector always had a kind word for me. If any of his brothers slagged me off, he'd shut them up. Priam, too, was like a father to me. He never displayed any resentment, even though the war cost him the lives of so many of his sons.

When Hector died, his pyre blazed all night. After extinguishing the dying embers with wine, his friends gathered up his ashes and placed them in a golden urn, which they wrapped in an embroidered purple cloth. Then they buried the urn and heaped a mound of stones on top.

The Greeks had kept their promise not to resume hostilities, but Priam wasn't taking any chances. He ordered sentries to be placed around the tomb. Such was the burial of Hector, tamer of horses, as Homer remarked at the end of the *Iliad*.

The Trojans managed to hold out for a few more months. With Hector gone, however, it was a doomed cause. Priam tried to stave off the inevitable by making alliances. One was with the Amazon queen, Penthesilea.

Penthesilea.

No fling was more momentary than the one Achilles had with her. Just when he thrust his spear into Penthesilea's breast (being an Amazon she had only one breast; that's the meaning of the word *amaza*, 'having only one breast'; Amazons cut off their left breast so that it doesn't get in the way when they shoot or hurl a spear) he fell hopelessly in love. She died instantly. Shortly afterwards Achilles was fatally shot in the heel by Paris. He'd got the short life he'd always craved.

I sometimes think I should have been an Amazon. Amazons hate men, you see, and I confess I've become a bit of a man-hater myself.

They devote themselves exclusively to war and use men solely for the purpose of reproducing themselves. They only raise girl babies. I won't tell you what they do with boy babies. It's too gruesome. On one occasion they launched an attack on Athens. They wanted to exact revenge on Theseus for having abducted an Amazon called Antiope. They encamped on the Areopagus and attacked the Acropolis, just like the Persians did hundreds of years later. Theseus defeated them, however, and to this day the Athenians commemorate this event.

Anyway, that all lies in the future. Troy fell not because of the superior prowess of the Greeks, nor because of their tactical superiority, nor because of their daredevil courage. It was due to trickery and deceitfulness. One day the Greek fleet sailed off. The Trojans assumed they'd given up all hope of taking their city. All that was left behind was a giant wooden horse.

The Trojans debated at length what to do with the horse. Some said it was a peace offering, others that it was a trap. While they were still at loggerheads, they discovered a Greek called Sinon. He claimed he'd been left behind because of Odysseus' enmity. He said the Greeks were hoping the Trojans would destroy the horse because that would arouse the anger of the gods.

Cassandra did her best to warn them. But as you know now, no one ever believed Cassandra's prophecies. Laocoön, a priest of Apollo, also tried to warn them. He threw his spear into the belly of the horse. You could actually hear the arms and armour inside rattle. Moments later, however, a sea monster slithered onto dry land and throttled Laocoön, along with his two sons.

The upshot was that the Trojans dragged the horse inside their city. The war was over, or so they thought. Everybody was celebrating and carousing. In the dead of night, when everyone was asleep, the Greek contingent inside the horse climbed out and threw open the gates to admit all their comrades, who had secretly returned.

Of course I have my regrets. Does anyone go through life without regrets? The war was a terrible thing. It didn't end with the fall of the city either. Once the Greeks had massacred all the males, including children and the elderly, they lined up the women and distributed them among themselves. It was all very democratic. Queen Hecuba was assigned to Odysseus as his slave.

On his way home to Ithaca, Odysseus stopped off in Thrace. Before the war broke out Hecuba and Priam had left their youngest son,

Polydorus, in the care of Polymestor, the local king and a longstanding guest friend of theirs. They'd entrusted him with gold to give to Polydorus in the event that the Trojans lost the war. Polymestor had murdered Polydorus as soon as Priam and Hector left.

Hecuba found all this out from the locals as soon as she landed in Thrace. She played innocent, however.

'Nice to see you, Polydorus,' she said, greeting him with a show of warmth. 'I hope my son didn't give you too much trouble. He can be a scallywag at times. It was kind of you to look after him. My husband has been killed and now I'm a slave. Where is the lad by the way? Pity he's not here to greet his old mother, although, truth to tell, it's probably for the best. I wouldn't want him to see me like this. Perhaps you and your boys could come over to my tent for a snack. Odysseus is only stopping over for the night. I got his permission to call on you.'

Polydorus tried to excuse himself but Hecuba wouldn't take no for an answer. Once she had him and his two sons inside, she showed her true colours. She struck Polydorus in both eyes and murdered his sons. Odysseus was horrified. Before he could do anything, however, one of the gods turned her into a dog. Can you blame her for what she did in view of all that she suffered? All her sons, her grandson, Astyanax, and her husband had been slaughtered.

Life has a way of turning out badly. That's been my experience. The gods are jealous and they do cruel things, often with absolutely no justification. Take the story of the mountain nymph, Echo, and her handsome lover, Narcissus. Echo was a chatterbox, so when Zeus wanted to muffle the sound of his lovemaking while he was bonking one of her sisters, he told Echo to engage Hera in conversation. At first Hera didn't suspect anything, but eventually she tired of Echo going on and on and told her to shut up. As soon as she did so, Hera heard her husband and his lover moaning in ecstasy. She punished poor Echo by condemning her to repeat the last words of the last person she had heard talking.

Narcissus soon tired of her after this, since she was incapable of saying anything original.

'I don't love you!' Narcissus shouted angrily.

Narcissus.

'Love you!' Echo echoed softly.

And so it continued, with Echo traipsing after her beloved, repeating his last words. One day, when he was walking in the countryside, Narcissus came to a lake surrounded by willow trees. Bending over the edge, he caught sight of his own image in the water. Instantly he fell in love. In fact he fell *so* much in love with himself that he began to pine away.

He thus became the progenitor of narcissistic personality disorder, while at the same time being transformed into a beautiful narcissus with its distinctive trumpet-shaped corona. Perhaps because he was always blowing his own trumpet.

It looks like I've got the last word. Here goes then.

May the words of those who have gone before you echo down the centuries until the ending of the world, world!

Plato

Any Greek was free to invent a myth, if she or he so chose. I certainly did, like this one about how we came to be bipeds. Originally there were three genders: male, female, and male/female known as hermaphrodites. They all had four arms, four legs, two faces attached to one head, and two sets of genitals. They were globular in shape, could walk backwards or forwards, and when they wanted to go fast they performed cartwheels. They were so arrogant, however, that they tried to storm Mount Olympus. Zeus was furious. He punished them by slicing them down the middle. Then he got Apollo to tie the loose bits together, knotting them together at the place we call our navel. That's how we came to have two arms, two legs, one head, and one set of genitals. It's also why we are all seeking our other half, so that we can become, literally, whole. And if we challenge Zeus again, he'll splice us down the middle a second time, and we'll have to go hopping on one leg. And perhaps if we're arrogant a third time, we won't have a leg to stand on.

I also invented a myth to explain the birth of Love. On the day that Aphrodite was born the gods were feasting on Mount Olympus. Resourcefulness, one of the guests, became drunk and wandered off into the garden, where he lay down and fell asleep. Poverty, who had been begging at the door of Zeus' palace to gain entry, snuggled down beside him and impregnated him while he was asleep. In time she gave birth to Love. This is why Love is both needy and resourceful. He's needy because lovers are always seeking the object of their desire, and he's resourceful because they go to great lengths to possess the object of their desire.

At the end of *The Republic*, Socrates tells the myth of Er the Pamphylian, who died in battle and came back to life just as he was about to be cremated.

Er suddenly sat up and described what he had witnessed down in Hades. After describing his experiences, Socrates says to his interlocutor, 'And so, Glaucus, the *mythos* was saved and did not perish, and if we pay attention to it, it might save us.'

Nothing that your modern culture has produced performs a similar function to the *mythos*, but if you pay attention to it, it might just save you.

Envoi

O Zeus and all you Olympians, if ever in the past you have harkened to my prayers, if ever you have received rich thigh pieces on the altar in my home, look favourably on those who read this book. Zeus, who inhabits the peaks of Mount Olympus, father of gods and men, son of Cronus, teach them justice and make them strong in fair dealing and honest practice. Hera, Queen of Heaven, favour them with the joys of companionship and like-mindedness. Athena, preserve them from the threat of war and guide them from the path of adversity. Dionysus, initiate them into the power of the irrational but do not let it turn their minds to fury and insanity. Aphrodite, cast your sweet glances upon them and instruct them in the joys of dalliance. Pythian Apollo, may the shafts of your arrows never pierce them with the pestilence. Artemis, chaste goddess of wild creatures, be not angry with them if they consecrate the marriage bed. Pan, most playful and amenable of all the gods, be beside them as they roam the wild. Poseidon, keep the seas and the skies safe for them. Demeter, grant abundance to all whom the broad-bosomed earth nourishes. Asclepius, saviour god, grant health and keep them pure in thought and deed. And Hermes, protector of travellers, be constantly at their side, till you accompany them, many years hence, on that last of all journeys upon earth's face.

Illustrations

All the illustrations are by the author. Most are inspired by Greek vases, others by Manga and Renaissance art.

Further reading

Aeschylus, *Agamemnon* (the murder of Agamemnon by his wife Clytemnestra).

Aeschylus, *Libation Bearers* (the revenge-killing of Clytemnestra by her son Orestes).

Aeschylus, *Eumenides* or *Friendly Ones* (the pursuit of Orestes by the Furies and his trial for the killing of his mother).

Apollodorus, *Library* (the most comprehensive collection of myths to survive from the ancient world).

Apollonius of Rhodes, *Argonautica* (Jason's search for the golden fleece; the most complete surviving treatment of any single myth).

Aristophanes, *Frogs* (the portrayal of Dionysus as an 'anti-hero', viz. cowardly, licentious, untrustworthy, and incontinent, and his descent to the Underworld).

Euripides, *Hippolytus* (Aphrodite's vengeance upon Hippolytus for his refusal to worship her).

Euripides, *Bacchae* (the opposition in Thebes to the cult of Dionysus, which results in the dismemberment of its king, Pentheus).

Hesiod, *Theogony* (the primordial deities and how the Olympians came into power).

Hesiod, *Works and Days* (Zeus as the upholder of justice and champion of the common people against the kings; the myth of the Five Ages).

Homer, *Iliad* (the final year of the Trojan War; Achilles' discovery that the world isn't just).

Homer, *Odyssey* (Odysseus' journey back home to Ithaca; Telemachus' coming of age).

Homeric Hymns (stories about the early days of the gods).

Ovid, *Metamorphoses* (Greek and Roman myths loosely bound together by the theme of shape-shifting).

Sophocles, *Oedipus the King* (the discovery by Oedipus that he has killed his father and married his mother).

Sophocles, *Antigone* (the refusal by Antigone to obey Creon's edict not to bury her brother Polyneices).

Sophocles, *Oedipus at Colonus* (the elevation to heroic status of the blind and aged Oedipus).